Born of Fire

A YEARLONG DIARY OF TRANSFORMATION

Deanna Cottrell

BALBOA.
PRESS
A DIVISION OF HAY HOUSE

Balboa Press books may be ordered through booksellers or by contacting:

Balboa Press
A Division of Hay House
1663 Liberty Drive
Bloomington, IN 47403
www.balboapress.com
1-(877) 407-4847

ISBN: 978-1-4525-4327-7 (sc)
ISBN: 978-1-4525-4328-4 (hc)
ISBN: 978-1-4525-4326-0 (e)
Library of Congress Control Number: 2011961417

Printed in the United States of America

Balboa Press rev. date: 12/07/2011

Dedicated to
Matthew Harold Waite
July 18, 1959 – May 6, 2010

Thanks to Janet Lembke for her editing expertise, her enduring friendship and unlimited patience. This book would not have been written without her. Thanks to my tea lady friends for their encouragement with this project, especially to Ellen Chase who kept after me to publish. Thanks to my brother, Gary, who funded this endeavor. His faith in my ability to get Born Of Fire in print has inspired me. Lastly, special thanks to all my friends and neighbors who have given their time, their love and care and their help along the way.

Deanna Cottrell

An Introduction

Your life implodes. Your marriage, which has lasted for a quarter of a century, is falling apart. Your budding career as a Polarity therapist, helping people to use their energy to create a life in harmony with nature, has been put on hold. Your body betrays you. Eye problems of unknown etiology cause periods of blindness. Your spiritual life, once a source of great strength, is sullied. The bed that you still share with your husband holds a third presence—the black goddess Kali, blood-stained consort of Shiva. What can you do? How can you save yourself?

These are the problems that Deanna Cottrell needed to surmount in order to find peace and, more than that, to keep her sanity. It would have been easy to give up, to make no decisions and just drift on the tides of other people's actions and desires. But she knew that she needed to find a transformative fire that would burn away her encumbrances and let true self shine forth. She wanted to become a phoenix rising in glory from the ashes. But, beset by impurities, many not of her own creation, she found it hard to find the spark that would ignite the healing conflagration.

Starting with November, a month of freezing cold, Born of Fire tells the stories of the year in which Deanna Cottrell sought and found fiery transformation. Deanna had experienced such transformations before, first with the birth of her four children, events that turned a naïve teenager into a mother with responsibilities far beyond herself.

And who had she been before she married and became a mother? Her family's oddball, that's who. Like many girls, she was horse-crazy.

Her means of coping with her failure to meet expectations turned her into a horse show-off. Her story is filled with wonderful accounts of her adventures with horsekind. She tells about her deep involvement in dressage with Salt My Luck, her American Quarter Horse, and about attending a school for equine massage, an experience that changed her life, when she was a grown woman. And she tells about her girlhood years of riding Duke, one of her grandmother's draft horses. Yes, big draft animals can buck. And, yes, they can be gentled for riding—except in drum-banging parades.

The year that Deanna Cottrell chronicles gives her a roller-coaster ride from the moment that she embarks on a journey of self-recovery, of healing a badly eroded identity. Making the decision to refresh and re-center herself, she leaves Vermont and her marriage temporarily and goes with her mother to her North Carolina retreat. Memories of her childhood in a fundamentalist family surface, from the dutiful church-going to unwelcome fondling by an uncle with a yen for girl-flesh. She recalls a horrific experience with fire: the burning of her grandmother's homestead, which had been her haven from unrealistic familial expectations. She recounts her adult conversion to a spiritual relationship with the natural world. Her newfound mantra is "How may I serve?"

When her husband joins her a month later, questions about the marriage are still unresolved, but she senses the presence of another woman. They both learn that the farmhouse that they rented in Vermont has been sold. Their new home will be an apartment in his office building, which he alone must fix up because her spells of blindness leave her unable to act. He leaves as the North Carolina spring is coming on, buds ready to explode. And he has given her a last present, a kayak that she'll use on the creek beside their southern home, the creek with brown, salty water in which she had been baptized several years earlier.

But, as the year undergoes its spring resurrection, the marital issues have not been resolved, and her come-and-go blindness worsens. She cannot drive or ride her bike, cannot paint because the colors are elusive, cannot even walk without a helping hand. But she's not alone, for her little dog and old cat are with her, needing food and love. The new kayak offers a refuge, for she can paddle with her eyes closed. Vigorous exercise helps. Still, she is trapped. When it seems that life cannot become bleaker, it does, with the arrival of a separation agreement taken out of a form book. She learns that the man to whom she is still married, though they are separated, is involved in an adulterous relationship.

Devastated, she asks, 'Who will love me? Who will want me? What can I do? Where will I go?" With the questions comes the realization that she has always let herself be defined by others. The only escape seems to be suicide. A phone call from a friend pulls her back from the abyss. And gradually she reaches out to some of the therapists whom she has met during her own training. She also seeks medical advice about her eyes. And, proud woman that she is, she learns to ask for help.

Help often comes to Deanna in unlooked for ways—a phone call when she's almost down and out, free meals brought from a local restaurant, the rallying around of her mother, son, and three daughters. Gradually, as the year rolls on, healing comes, though not without hard work. After a year of dismissal by doctor after doctor—your eye problems are caused by stress or heavy-metal poisoning, she finally receives a diagnosis and a means of alleviating the uncontrollable spasms that close her eyes. Meditating, praying, joining other women for the sacred cleansing in a sweat lodge, she tends with ferocity to her spiritual life. Memory, too, plays a part, sending her back to the happy times—horses, building her North Carolina home, and sailing with her husband. Most important, friends and family extend the love she yearns for, and her emotions find peace. Healing is not something that can be accomplished wholly in solitude.

Though our circumstances may be different from Deanna Cottrell's, many of us have found ourselves in Deanna Cottrell's place, our worlds falling apart. Where do we go? What can we do? This book of hope and transformation is for us.

Janet Lembke,

Janet Lembke is the author of twenty books on the natural world, end of life issues, and cooking

NOVEMBER

With stammering lips and insufficient sounds,
I strive and struggle to deliver right
The music of my nature.

E.B.BROWNING

I lie awake early in the predawn darkness contemplating if I should get out of my warm nest to meditate or continue to snuggle in with my thoughts. I sense the raw November cold outside the window overlooking the sweeping lawn and on down to the shore of Lake Bomoseen, Vermont. There is a good chance that I will catch a glimpse of the small deer herd browsing on the downed acorns that were shed by the ancient oaks a few weeks ago. I especially like to watch the deer in the moonlight. But the moon is dark now. My thoughts roll on through my mind like ocean waves rolling in on a sandy shore. Gently they roll in, wash up on the beach of my consciousness, and then wash back out disappearing into the vast sea of thought. Just yesterday, I walked with my dog, Duffy, a Welsh Terrier, along the lakeshore. There were large holes of open water especially on the north shore. The ducks have gathered here for their last watering hole until they are forced to leave to seek open water elsewhere. They cling to each last oasis of open water in the vast pool of frozen whiteness. They fly to a hole, then swim to the icy edge, which is just slush right now. Then they push their way through the mushy ice to the next hole leaving behind a trail, which will freeze in intricate lacy patterns like follow-the-dot drawings.

I drift to my work and my studies. I am very tired and having a difficult time energizing myself to fulfill my busy schedule. My classes at the Polarity Realization Institute where I have been learning and practicing Polarity Energy Balancing and Healing for the past year and a half are now winding down for the winter months. I will postpone a few classes as I have before during the winter so that I may spend time at our home in North Carolina after the first of the year. However, this year will be different, as I have to come back for a class in March, an Anatomy and Physiology exam and a six-week internship thereafter. Ah, North Carolina, my refuge, the place where I go to feed my hungry soul, to settle and balance my mind, rejuvenate my body, and paint. I began drawing and painting when I was a young girl. After my marriage and the subsequent births of my four children, I painted feverishly into the night as a way to hold onto reality and my sense of self. Later, I was able to take lessons from a local artist by the name of Trudy Lewis who was from New York. She and her husband, Kenneth who was a physician, had moved to Vermont a few years earlier. I studied with Trudy for several years once a week in the evening when my husband was home to baby-sit. Not only did I learn the mechanics of oil painting from Trudy but also self-expression. She taught me how to see the world through the eyes of an artist. The basis for my own teaching style came from those early lessons with Trudy. One of the techniques she taught us was to paint several coats of under color before bringing in any details of the composition. As a result, the depth of color in the painting is intensified. One of the reasons I went to North Carolina for the winter back in 1989 was to have time alone to paint. Of course, the other reason was for the warmth. I feel a rush of that sweet warmth through my limbs as this memory of sunshine and light passes through my mind.

> *In the words of Land Otter,*
> *I call you, Northwest Wind,*
> *That you may come and help me,*
> *And blow me to the where I am going.*

Again, a mind shift back to my rigorous schedule and I contract again in coolness. I have been driving back and forth from Vermont to Ipswich, Massachusetts, and Portland, Maine, each week, sometimes twice a week since early spring. The driving amounts to about a thousand miles a week. I still have two classes to take before I escape southward with the ducks. My life has become much like the ducks' life in November. I search for open water for survival and creativity in the vastness of frozen relationship. I cling to my work, to my spiritual practice, my children and grandchildren, my artwork, and my studies. My twenty-five year marriage has become nearly frozen and maintaining the holes in the ice becomes increasingly challenging. I continually swim between them trying frantically to keep the pathways clear and the holes open, balanced and connected. I feel worn and weary. My eyes have been burning and itching for a few months especially while I am driving. After seeing a few doctors, who suggested a mild dry eye condition and prescribed artificial tears, I have continued to push myself on towards my clearly defined but multiple goals. I am a juggler; the balls, my practice, my studies, completing the internship in the spring of '98, attending a Cranial Sacral Retreat in Burlington, Vermont, this month just before Thanksgiving, planning and hosting our family Thanksgiving feast, Christmas preparations and packing up to move south for four months. I struggle to hold myself together and to thaw some of the ice that has crept into my marriage.

As though he senses my thoughts, the body in the bed next to me stirs and my mind comes face to face with the challenge ahead. How to keep this marriage from becoming totally frozen out where we must both fly away to survive? At this time, there is only a small hole open in the icy vastness of years of emotional abuse punctuated by moments of pure sunlit bliss and joy. We had met years before when I attended a business law class he was teaching at a local college. I actually had taken an immediate dislike to Joe as a professor but I had heard that he was an excellent attorney. But in the class atmosphere, he seemed to me to be arrogant and demeaning especially to the women. He brought out feelings of anger in me that I hadn't been aware of before. After the class finished, I met him a couple of times over the next few years as he helped my husband and me with some legal matters. Then in the early

'70s as my first marriage was about to dissolve, I hired him to represent me. We met several times during the process, I saw a different Joe, and the relationship grew.

We were both romantics. He sent flowers, gifts, wrote poetry and songs for me throughout our courtship and the early years of marriage. We had a shared passion for our home, our family and travel. We loved our home and the 100 acres of land our home sat on. We eagerly shared it with family and friends on a regular basis. We lived and played in this wonderfully spacious house for 11 years before downsizing to a townhouse.

We both brought much baggage to this second marriage. I brought a lifetime of dependence on a male figure in my life to financially support me as well as four teenage children. He brought two younger children along with a family background of dishonesty, emotional pain and addiction. Our families blended together as one during the vacations they shared at our hillside homestead in Vermont. There was more joy during those years than pain. We swam, hiked, fished, water-skied and rode our horses during the summers. Then we skied, slid and snowmobiled all winter. In the autumn there was wood to cut, split and stack to feed three hungry wood burning stoves that heated our home. We had three dogs, a cat, two horses and for a short time, two hogs. There were always extra kids coming and going. Sometimes it was hard to tell who was who in that dynamic house of continuous movement and life. Summers and school vacations were particularly chaotic when my husband's two children joined us.

We had a share in a boat which we kept on Lake Bomoseen. All of our six children skied behind that boat at one time or another. We enjoyed sunset crises visiting with many neighbors who had homes on the shore of the Lake. Often in the heat of the summer, we would take cocktails and snacks as well as a few friends out for a cruise, then end up at one of the restaurants located on the shore where we could dock the boat. The children all learned to fish from that old boat called the Sunshine. Our youngest son was passionate about fishing so much that we told him he was catching way over the allowable limit and the game warden would probably catch up with him. Our goal was to cool his enthusiasm enough to allow us some breathing time in between fishing trips. Imagine our son's surprise and our shock when the game warden appeared at our door the next day. It turned out it was totally unrelated but the sight of that uniformed man at our door sent our youngest son into hiding.

My mind drifts to our Thanksgiving feast coming in just two weeks. How we have grown and changed! I make a mental tally of those who will be attending this year. It appears to be thirty-one at this count, one of the largest celebrations we have ever had. All of our children and grandchildren will be together with the exception of our youngest son. Last year we were a large group as well but there were a few family members missing. How fortunate we are to have rented this big old farmhouse on the lake. It is truly a gift from God. I knew it the first time we saw it but there was something else that I couldn't quite grasp at the time. A preciousness, a need to share our togetherness here as much as possible, a treasury of memories to be made in a short time. This was to be an interim home as it was for sale and it would probably be only a matter of a couple of years before it was sold. I realized this gift only as a temporary one as most gifts are and therefore all the moments I spent there sharing with my loved ones were very precious. We have opened this house as much as possible to family gatherings in the year and a half since we moved in. The house can almost be heard to sing with the joy of it. We came here in July 1996 after selling our city townhouse in March of that year. Since then, we have lived with children, on our boat and finally in a motel until this house was gifted to us by our Creator.

I am inwardly drawn to the Earth-based religion of the Native Americans. I come by it naturally I guess, since one of my great great grandmothers was a Native American from the Iroquois Nation, probably Mohawk or Seneca. There is an ever-present awareness of totem animals and signs from the Earth that will lead me along the path that will provide the lessons I am here to learn. Animals appear in our awareness to teach us and accompany us if we just listen and observe. The bear has been a totem animal for me for a few years. I have seen them from time to time in my garden in Vermont and along the roads of North Carolina.

5

The very first night we spent here in this old farmhouse, a full moon shone. Our sister moon was illuminating the entire first floor with her cool white light, breathtakingly beautiful as she sparkled and danced on the water. In the early morning, I heard the poignant call of the loons. My heart sang and I smiled at the welcome sight of a pair of loons in the cove directly in front of the house. I knew then that this was right where I belonged for now. The loon has also been my totem sign, teaching me to breathe deeply and go within myself to do the spiritual inner work that will provide the nourishment for my soul. The presence of a loon always causes me to dream more vividly and to remember who I am and why I am here.

Ted Andrews in his book, *Animal Speak*, describes the loon totem as teaching us to breathe deeply to enable us to enter into "varying degrees of consciousness, while maintaining control." This may reflect the potential for us to become more conscious in our dream state. "The haunting call of the loon may also be telling you that all of those hopes, wishes, and dreams that you have tucked to the back of the heart are about to come to the surface."

The cold creeps in the bedroom as dawn approaches and I snuggle deeper into my blankets knowing I must soon scramble out and make a dash for the warmth of the downstairs sunroom. I will join my husband in meditation, a morning ritual we have been able to share for about a year. I cling with hope to this small time of sharing.

It is often at this hour of the morning that I am awakened, especially during periods of high stress. My mind, eager to organize my "do list," begins running through one job after the other planning my day and the following day as well if I allow it. Trying to just be and stay in the moment during times of busy-ness is truly challenging.

So much of my life has been devoted to being the super-mom of this family, a position I learned and reluctantly accepted many years ago as a young bride and parent. In those days, father's provided the income for the family but were not very involved in the day to day rearing of children especially four small children about a year apart. That period was also a major transformative period in my life. Having never been involved with the care of infants or even young children, the birth of my first child was a shock. I was completely unprepared and unequipped to care for a newborn infant. I had never been allowed to have babysitting jobs as my older sister had. The reason may have been that I was fearful to stay alone in our house so my parents decided I could not care for other children. I was a tomboy and didn't pay much attention to anything that went on inside the house except for cooking. Cooking was a form of creative expression from an early age, one that my grandmother helped to expand with her lessons. But as for parenting, I was not much more than a child myself. I was a month and a half short of my nineteenth birthday when my son was born. The other three children came along in the next five years. The child I was, was cast into the fire of transformation to emerge a mother.

Fire transforms whatever it touches. It is the only element that can do that completely. Fire is destructive as well as creative. It purifies and it burns away the dross so that the gold can shine forth. It is the mystery of the Phoenix who rises from the ashes. Fire is the element of the heart, the center of our passion and our love; it can help us to recreate our lives. It is the element of regeneration and resurrection. In the Native American tradition, prayers are offered to the six directions. They call on Great Spirit, Earth Mother and the four directions of the compass each time they pray or do ceremony. They recognize and honor Mudjekeewis, Spirit Keeper of the West, Grandfather of All The Winds. The element associated with Mudjekeewis is fire. The animal honored in the west is the grizzly bear who teaches healing through introspection and quiet. The thunder beings also reside in the west. The west is honored in the Medicine Wheel, the sacred hoop or circle of life, as the place of autumn and vibrant colors. Here is the opportunity to gather our harvest, whether it is a moment, a day, a year or a lifetime. This is the time to sort through the chaff or dross of our lives by going deep within through meditation and the study of our dream work thereby revealing the finest golden radiance of our spirit. It is a time of deep introspection, dreaming, rest and contemplation. Fire is the one element that produces a total transformation.

I was fascinated by fire as a child. I begged to be allowed to carry out the trash so I could burn the papers and make campfires out in the yard. I built fires like the ones I saw in the cowboy movies I loved so much. I then would put a can on a stick and boil leaves and grasses to make a "meal" or "tea." Hours were spent in joyful fantasy. Little did I know that my journey through life would be highlighted many times by the power of fire.

After I had been cast into the fire as a young woman by the births of my four children, the dross was burned away and what began to emerge was a strong, purposeful matriarchal figure that thought she could hold it all together by her will alone. Oh, I prayed to God for help during those times of fear. Sometimes I even took the time to give thanks too but usually that was prior to asking for help. It was a polite way of asking for God's assistance. Miraculously, those frantic prayers were usually answered and my faith in the God of last resort was sustained. More often than not, it was my faith in myself that was shored up and strengthened. The woman who emerged from the fire was very different from the girl who was tossed in.

"When I first came here, when I was born.
I brought the most wonderful lizard knowledge with me;
I brought a wild, strong cold-blooded passion.
I knew how to walk in this place.
I knew precisely where to place my feet
but my mother and my father were shocked
and wondered where I came from.
When I first came here,
I wondered who I was and my parents
Questioned where I fit in.
And they all wondered what to do.
So I went deep underground and found a temporary face
that could get me through until I
could escape to a new place.

That poem by Emily Amonett which I have paraphrased, closely describes my early journey in this life with my family. I had always been told I was different from the rest of the family. Everything I tried to do was excused as being the product of my eccentric nature, so just let her be. It seemed that no matter how I tried I could never conform to my family's expectations. I became a show-off on horses because it seemed the perfect way for me to receive the attention I craved as well as satisfying my need for non-conformity. I often brought the horse down to my parent's home and raced around the yard, rearing and galloping dangerously about. When I became a young teen, I shaved my eyebrows off and had my long wavy hair cut in what was called at that time, The Italian Boy Cut. My mother was shocked by my appearance but it was my way of forcing them to see me as something other than, "the pretty one". Mama told me she had once entered me in a beauty pageant as an infant. She also reminded me a few times that I had not won. As I grew older, I continued to feel as though I was always outside watching rather than participating in life. All through my school years, I spent much time trying to learn to conform to what I thought my peers and my family wanted rather than discovering who I really was. For me as always, one need stood out clearly, that was the desire to help others especially animals.

My self-image was poor therefore when I was introduced, at age 14 at an ice skating party on a nearby pond, to a young man nearly 8 years my senior, I was thrilled beyond words. His name was Mac and he had just mustered out of the US Navy. He drove a brand new red Ford with glass pack mufflers and fender skirts. He had traveled the world over on an aircraft carrier. He swept me off my giddy young feet until a few weeks later when he realized my age. He disappeared from my life for a month. Unable to get me off his mind and reconciled with my age, he returned. With my parents approval, we dated for the next four years. It was understood and expected by everyone that we would marry when I came of age. All my youthful dreams were suffocated in that smoldering fire. My terrible need to be noticed and appreciated far outweighed my self-expression for the next four years. By the time I came to realize and honor who I was, I had been married to this man and birthed four children. Eleven more years passed. It took all the courage I could muster to end that marriage and move on.

I dreamed of becoming a veterinarian. My grandmother often told me she would support me to reach that goal but when the time came to do so, the money she had put away for my education was gone. Then, of course, I had plenty to nurture with the births of my children and the animals that we kept. My husband and I always had pigs, rabbits, beef cattle and horses on our mini-farm.

The pattern continued when I became a real estate broker and then later a bank officer. I was caring for people and their specific needs, namely home, auto and finances. My primary objective when I was in banking was sales. Yes, I ran a small branch but the reason I was hired was because of my background in sales. As it turned out, I was able to increase the branch deposits by three-hundred percent before I resigned. Later, I taught a group of senior citizens and many children drawing and oil painting for several years. When I reached the half-century mark in my life, it was only natural for me to want to continue in a helping profession.

Now there is a menu to plan, groceries to buy, pies to make, tables to set up and a thirty-pound turkey to be picked up, stuffed and roasted in the predawn hours of Thanksgiving Day. Each family attending will bring a contribution to the dinner so the cooking chores have been reduced from the early years when the responsibility was totally mine.

My mind skips on to the Cranial Sacral Retreat in Burlington, Vermont, initiated by two of my former Polarity teachers. I am planning to attend for five days this week. I am anticipating a relaxing and spirit-filled period of learning and healing. I will be with a select group of my peers and teachers. The facility, which will house us for the week is part of the Episcopal Diocese and is located on the shores of Lake Champlain in a lovely private wooded place. Cranial Sacral work was originally the vision of Dr. Andrew Taylor Still in 1874. He had a vision that healing should begin with the bones. If the mechanism was in proper structural alignment, it would function perfectly. Dr. Still was the father of manipulative medicine. He was a Union soldier and traveled throughout the Midwest where he founded College of Osteopathy in Kirksville, Mo. Dr. Still was known as the Old Doctor.

Dr. Sutherland followed in early 1900's. He further discovered that the cranial sutures were moveable. Dr. Sutherland spent twenty years experimenting with Cranial Movement. He applied Dr. Still's principles and Philosophy of Osteopathy to the cranium. He found the body is a whole unit; each part affects the other and felt the body could heal itself. He believed the brain was God's pharmacy. Thirty years passed before he shared his research with other doctors. Dr. Sutherland wrote under the name of "Blunt Bone Bill". He was treated with disdain and rejection by his peers. A few brave doctors finally did send him patients they could not heal. There still existed resistance during the 1930's. In the 40's, people began to listen. The Denver County Osteopaths began to follow Dr. Sutherland's methods. Howard and Rebecca Lippincott were some of the first osteopaths he trained in cranial sacral therapy. During the late '40s and '50s, he trained others. Dr. Sutherland passed away in 1954, in his eighties. The Sutherland Cranial teaching foundation still exists today. At the end of his career, he talked about the Breath of Life, the life force or the movement of the Cranial Sacral Fluid. Cerebrospinal (CS) fluid stores and conveys life energy or Prana. The source of this energy is consciousness itself. When we gain access to this very source of life energy, we are able to resource the greatest power of healing. It is the liquid medium of the Life Force, expanding and contracting in a rhythm all its own. When this CS fluid is flowing openly and unobstructed within the spine, then life and healing with normal function will be present. When there is an obstruction, spasm, stagnation or pain, then there is a reduction of Life Force, leaving the person unable to live fully. The Cranial Sacral work will enhance and expand all the previous training I have had and enable me to offer more options to my clients.

"Then the Lord God formed man of the dust of the ground,
and breathed into his nostrils the Breath of Life;
and man became a living soul." Genesis 2:7

I have been pushing myself relentlessly to finish Polarity school. The work involves building my practice and teaching seminars while struggling with a faltering marriage, all the time trying to maintain my spiritual practice. My life seems out of control. I know it but there still exists the illusion that I alone can somehow make it work and bring it all back to balance. If I pray long enough, stay focused on loving thoughts and work hard enough, it will somehow come to balance.

Shortly after I lie down for a nap, I experience a powerful dream. I am standing on a transformer in an electrical power plant surrounded by a crowd of children of all ages. The older children are holding the infants; the toddlers cling to the legs of the older ones. I am speaking to them, assuring them, teaching them quietly when suddenly we are all propelled by an incredible force out of the plant up into the air. We fly directly upward with a force that strains our bodies. I feel the vastness and the power of the universe, while still feeling the connectedness with all there is. As I glance to my left and my right, I see we are flying together in a v formation, our faces strained with the force of the flight, arms at our sides. As suddenly as we took off, we are stopped and in that moment of hesitation, we are propelled downward with equal force guiding us back to the Earth. We enter the ocean and I feel the rush of the salty water on my face and eyes as we surge to the center of Earth where we stand together in a wonderful warm red chamber. I have barely time to glance around before I am off again upward towards the heavens once more. This time as I glance to my right side, I see I am accompanied by a seven-year-old male child. Everyone else was left safely behind. We stop and I ask him what it is he needs. He informs me he is seeking nurturing, attention and love. I hold him close and open my heart to him. He tells me he wishes to be with Grandmother Sarah so I deliver him to her. As I am whisked away, I am given the vision of that young male part of myself joyously clinging to her waist. As I fly on, suddenly the force increases in power and speed. I look ahead and see an ancient forest of tall redwood trees. Humorously, I think, "Oh, this is going to hurt" as I hurtle towards the trees. As I collide with the trees, there is an intense explosion of light, color and sound. I burst into a billion fragments of Light and become one with the universe.

The ego is very reluctant to give up control to our higher selves and will cause us to cling to our illusions especially in times of worldly stress and busyness. The big "I" was still in charge even though I constantly professed to have given control of my life over to God. I still hung onto that rapidly shredding thread of control and fear. During meditation I was given an image of curtains made of fine fabric hung on a rod of golden Light. As the opening to the other realms grows larger, there is extra fabric for allowances and errors. I am ready to open to another dimension but need to learn discernment before that is possible; otherwise the whole thing could unravel. Over the course of the next six years, I was given what I like to call my "D" word lessons during meditation. Words such as: Discover, discipline, dedication, detachment, and discernment. After receiving one of these words, I would meditate on it for a lengthy period of time until it became apparent to me what it meant to me and how I was to apply it to my life. I think these words are lessons for me to complete as I move along this path. I will revisit the "D" word lessons many times in years to come.

My dream state is active and vivid with images of what is to transpire in the coming year but I don't fully understand the nightly revelations at this time. At one point, I dreamed I already knew how to fall gracefully and come up unharmed. Then I am in an old house. The floors are weak and full of holes. I fall through into a dirty shower but the water doesn't work. Scary people keep coming and going. I am afraid they will get into my room. A large threatening woman with a shield enters and says she is going to beat me up and there will be blood. I know there are drastic changes ahead. The thought has crossed my mind that I am going to die. Actually, that prospect is appealing rather than frightening not only because of my spiritual beliefs but because I am so tired, stressed and rapidly losing my grip on the illusion of control.

I was naked in the dream, holding onto my husband's arm, always going here and there. I saw nothing wrong with it. It is what I am. I am a naked object, a prostitution of my true self. There are a group of children staring at me and suddenly I realize the truth just as the emperor did in the story of the Emperor's New Clothes. I am so ashamed. I run away.

My eyes are very dry and itchy. It is all I can do to keep them open especially when I enter a vehicle. It is increasingly difficult to drive any distance. I pull the car over to the side of the road to grab a nap thinking that is what I need but as soon as the car stops and I close my eyes for a few moments, I find I am wide awake and anxious to move on. Well-meaning friends continue to offer many suggestions but what seems to provide some relief is chewing or singing as loudly as I can. I carry a rather large supply of snack foods, the cache size determined by the length of the trip. As my eye condition worsens so does my weight soar in proportion. In an attempt to project his own fears of aging on me, my husband chides me about my weight gain as well as the fact that I no longer dye my rapidly graying hair. I recall our last sailing trip together in July when he blurted out his feelings about my appearance.

The last time we sailed together aboard our sailboat, *Nepenthe,* was July, 1997. *Nepenthe* was a thirty-six foot fiberglass sloop made in Maine. We had purchased her about ten years earlier and had spent many happy times aboard her. It was customary for us to take a week the early part of July and sail up or down Lake Champlain revisiting familiar places while exploring new ones. It was an adventure we both looked forward to each year. Sometimes we were able to carve out another week in the latter part of the summer but most of the time we limited our sailing to every weekend. We had decided to sail leisurely northward towards Canada.

As stormy weather approached, we put into Plattsburgh Yacht Basin on the New York side of the Lake. After settling in, we sat down facing one another on the settees and finally began to speak openly and honestly with one another. I was grateful for an honest exchange at last, after much silence or hedging on the subject. He said he felt like I was his mother in our dialogues. He felt my powerful spirit and was intimidated by it. Then he said he had memories of the way I looked in the past as a younger person and how I've put on weight and how and how and now—I listened carefully, I accepted his honesty, but my heart closed down. We spent the rest of the day doing what we do in port on a stormy day. We played scrabble as the storms rolled through. I beat him soundly, a rare occurrence. He was angry with himself, he blamed the letters, and he blamed me.

We went off to the movies to see Julia Roberts in *My Best Friend's Wedding;* it was quite good. We decided to walk the distance from the cinema in the mall to an Italian restaurant. After the movie, he charged from the theater, stopped to ask for directions, and then charged onward. The image of me trotting along behind was not lost on me as it always seemed that has been my position with this man for much of our twenty-five year marriage. There I am, stumbling, tumbling along behind him. I felt the anger and resentment rising in my throat. There was a great deal of pain in my abdomen and solar plexus. My heart was still closed from our earlier discussion. I picked up the pace and stepped along with him. He went faster so I decided to stay with him if it took all I had. We burst out the doors of the mall, each to his own door. I silently wished I had worn my sneakers rather than my clogs. By now, I was breathing rapidly. I gritted my teeth and decided, I will not allow him to cut me off, nor will he sway me from my path. I watched him out the sides of my eyes; he was a man with a mission. He strode easily for a man with short legs. I have long legs but I had to run to keep up with him. As we went on, I became breathless and tearful. I was so frustrated. I kept repeating over and over to myself, why do we have to do this? Why must we race from one place to another, never cherishing the journey? I finally dropped back as suddenly as I had sprinted forward with him. I realized at that moment that I could no longer walk with him. The journey is over! Our paths separated and I was given total pure insight. I saw how far apart we had moved and the lack of respect, compassion and love we felt for one another. The whole picture was revealed to me as if I was watching a movie script. We were seated and served before I could speak. I was unable to finish my dinner, the food seemed to stick in my throat and swallowing was impossible. The pain in my lower chakras (energy vortices located in the abdomen and the pelvis) had become so intense by this time, that I excused myself and headed to the rest room to clear the heavy sticky energy that had engulfed me.

The previous two years, he had been representing a divorce client in a bitter and hateful process. As often happens in life, our lessons or challenges come in multiples. He was confronted with issues including not only our relationship, but also the relationship with his own family members, in addition to the representation of a client who mirrored many of the same issues. This amounted to a painful crunching "bring him to his knees" type of lesson. I like the image of an athlete who must crouch down deeply to center himself, and then pull in all his energies so he can make a powerful leap upward. Sometimes when one is dealing with these strong lessons, it is as though we are being shaken by the shoulders and told to face up rather than just the gentle tap on the shoulder that reminds us we need to listen. I felt he had become terrified of the aging process in himself and in struggling fearfully

15

with various physical ailments; he projected his fear on me. He had reached out for some thread of spirituality through vain attempts at meditation and prayer. Meanwhile, his anger and resentment grew and was spent on me. The more he could dump on me, the lighter his load would be temporarily. Then it would build up again and the same process would be repeated. I was having great difficulty functioning in our relationship. It all seemed out of sync. There was definitely a lack of respect, admiration, friendship and love. It had become almost impossible for me to remain loving and appreciative in this union.

Loving-kindness was seen as my weakness and I allowed the yo-yo behavior in our marriage. Many times with alcoholism, the drinking stops but the behaviors continue as before. He ran from his real life challenges by throwing himself into other people's problems to the extent that his own need and the needs of his wife were often neglected. I continued to pray for him and surround him in white light. Perhaps a separation for the month of January will propel both of us to work more diligently towards positive growth. We are alike in at least one way, which is we don't know our own honest heart feelings. When we do listen to our hearts, we don't know how to honor those feelings. We have denied ourselves for so many years, that we don't know who we really are. It is almost like accepting a wardrobe from some stranger. We try on the things, they seem to fit at first due to our excitement over their newness but then we realize that these clothes are not right for us so then we try on some other things. What is real? Where is the honesty? We had ridden this emotional roller coaster together for two years while we both began a transformative healing crisis.

We left the restaurant in a huff. Once outside, he began to hound me about how I have ruined a great day. I said little as a feeling of peace and calmness had replaced my earlier panic. I did note the sun was out and it was clear at last. It was very lovely, the rain had stopped. I smiled and said; "Life is about opposites, contrasts and polarity isn't it?" When we got to the boat after a silent taxi ride, I told him it was over. I could not suffer this pain anymore. I told him I was tired of his excuses for everything he did or said.

The boat is damp and as I bent to pull on my socks for sleeping, I caught the only fingernail I had left in the scab of a rope burn I had received a few days earlier as a result of being tangled up with my daughter's dog. The scab came off and the wound bled profusely. How appropriate I thought. I needed to bleed at that time. Bleeding and birthing, painful but productive pain. I will birth my true self at last. No more sway, push, pull, and run after, just me as I am, maybe fat, maybe thin, white hair, no makeup if I choose, me, just me! Productive pain, I knew this pain, it was familiar. I can take it. No more destructive, useless pain, nagging, sucking out my life force. And so the birthing begins. The following day was Independence Day, July 4, 1997.

In the meantime, I continue to sense the presence of other women, real or mythological, in my marriage. One night in New Hampshire as we stayed over with a friend, I met one such woman face to face.

We had attended an anniversary party for a couple of friends and rather than drive back at such a late hour, we slept over at our friend's house. During the night, I was awakened by a chill and realized that my husband had gathered most of the blankets over to his side of the bed. As I sat up to tug on them in an attempt to cover myself, a dusty black woman sat up between us. She looked deep into my eyes and I let out a scream. She screamed at the same time and then took her leave. My shriek awakened my husband, who thought I had been dreaming. I don't think he quite believed me when I told him what I had witnessed. It was many months before I realized that the dusty black woman in my bed between my husband and me was the Hindu Goddess Kali.

Kali, a warrior goddess, is the most realized of all the Dark Goddesses. She is the Goddess of Death, destruction and transformation. She is called by many names, Parvati being one. Parvati being more gentle and of a motherly nature. Durga is the Goddess who spawned her from her own brow during a battle with demons. Her very appearance is meant to terrify with her many arms and necklace of skulls. She was the consort of the God Shiva and as such encouraged and provoked him to disruptive, anti-social behavior. She is at home outside the moral order and seems to be unbounded by that order. In a poem by Mel Lyman, he writes of Kali's threat to burn down our world, tear down everything that cannot stand alone. Destroy our ideals and reduce everything to rubble after which she will burn the rubble and scatter the ashes. Kali's intent is to show us the way things really are with no illusions. As I said, it took many months for me to process my meeting with Kali. If I had understood more clearly at the time of her visit, perhaps I would have been better prepared for what I was to face in the next couple of years.

This process of transformation could be called a Trial by Fire but I prefer to think of it as a Transformation by Fire. I had after all been born to this life in the fire of the Aurora Borealis. The darkness of the night of my birth was illuminated by the Northern Lights, the fire in the sky. Those who remember say it was the most spectacular show of light they had ever witnessed. Many people were terrified that it pronounced the coming of the end of the world. In panic their telephone calls jammed radio stations, police stations and the clergy offices. The people in the little bedroom of my father's house were also very fearful of the future and there they were with a new life in their midst. As I came into this dimension from the warmth and safety of my mother's womb, I too felt the bitter taste of fear and resisted coming out. I sensed my mother's fear as she pushed me out into the arms of my grandmother. My father was away in Indiana picking up a new fire truck for the town and arrived home about the same time I arrived.

As the days passed, I was unable to shake the fear that had permeated my initiation into this life and decided to return from whence I came. My breath was shallow from fear and my lungs began to fill with fluid. I was unable to breathe fully the breath of life and soon developed a full-blown case of pneumonia. I hovered on the brink of death for many hours. Guidance in the form of angels came to me and instructed me to stay. I was reminded of the tasks and the lessons I had come to complete in this life. In addition, I felt such concern from my family, such love, such caring and compassion that I made the decision to stay and grow.

Suddenly I am brought out of my barely conscious state as my husband jumps from the bed, pulls on sweats and slippers and heads downstairs to the warmth of the sunroom. I follow shortly and find that he has a candle lit and is already seated facing the south and the lake. I sit down in my chair, light a candle and face the east. Soon the first rays of the sun will burst forth over the low trees and hills bathing me with its blessed golden warmth and light. I am given another opportunity for rebirth, refreshment and resurrection. I call on Wabun, Spirit Keeper of the East. The east is springtime, refreshment, renewal, rebirth and resurrection. The animal associated with the east is the eagle. The eagle provides us with the larger picture from its great height. It is here that we greet our Father Sun each day.

The Cranial Sacral retreat provides me with an opportunity to step back in clarity from my headlong dash through my present life. The high energy of being surrounded by other healers, giving and receiving the healing work throughout the day has a powerful cleansing effect on my system. Throughout the day we take turns holding each other's heads and sacrum's, feeling the breath of life and the rhythm of the cranial sacral fluid. The evenings are spent meditating in front of a roaring fire. Usually after an early morning meditation and yoga, I find time for a brisk walk through the snow covered fields and rock strewn paths. I make my way carefully down to the lake shore until cold fingers, frozen cheeks and nose bring me back to the prospect of a warm mug of tea laced with honey.

It is quite appropriate that this deep introspection would present itself to me in the autumn of the year and in the autumn of my physical life. I have learned from my lessons with Native American teachers to celebrate and honor the four directions of the winds as well as The Creator and Mother Earth. As I said earlier in this chapter, the west is a time of autumn, a time of deepening darkness and contraction inward. It is a time to rest, to contemplate, and to reap the harvest of the past year's crops, to gather in what we have sown, to sort through the bounty to discover the heart and soul of it all. As we gather the harvest, we inspect it then burn away all the dross or chaff, the impurities to reveal the gold or the heart that comes from a day, a year or a lifetime of planting and nurturing.

Midweek of the retreat, I realize I cannot go on as I have been. I need to figure out how best to do my service and honor whom I serve without the strain on my system. It is quite clear to me at this time, that I serve only the expectations of others and of my ego self. I know I must go home and face my relationship issues head on but I don't know how. I know I cannot drive myself in the advanced Polarity program any longer. The toll has been too great to warrant any further energetic expense. I have come to a full halt, faced with major decisions and possible changes but I feel freer and lighter that I have in months.

> "The most vulnerable time for new truth in our lives
> is immediately after the discovery.
> Like the emerging seedling,
> we have made the decision to leave the seed's protective shell."
> From *Deep Water Passage* by Ann Linnea

I pray and meditate morning and night for the strength and guidance to help me make the right choices, say the proper words and yet be true to my deepest self. My dear friend and counselor, Nicky, is there for me. After months of friendship and a deep soul connection, she knows me on a level that I have never shared with anyone. Symbolically, she drives me to get my summer tires removed from my car and replaced by my four knobby snow treads, so that I do not get stuck or slide off my path in the muck and ice that is to come.

As I leave the retreat, I know my life is about to change. I feel I have made a huge step forward in just listening and honoring the voice within. After cutting the class in Maine, it is time to talk with my husband. I pray for the appropriate words to come as I share my thoughts and insights. I need time to rest and rejuvenate. I want to work on our marriage but I cannot do so in this exhausted state of body, mind and spirit. I must pull out of the Polarity program for a while at least. As it is, I need only thirty-five credit hours to complete it. After talking with Nicky, it is decided that I will self-design and direct the remaining courses with her mentoring my progress.

Upon returning from the Cranial Sacral Retreat, my husband and I discuss my need for space and quiet time to recover my health and rejuvenate my spirit. My eyes are very dry now. I feel as though there are twigs, hair and even red pepper in them. I am forced to cut way back on my driving. I can no longer drive the hour and a half to see my mother without major stress. I ask Joe to give me some time alone in North Carolina throughout January and February. As it turns out, my mother will be with me for that time and I am uncertain of my ability to care for her as well as myself. Due to the depth of my fatigue, I don't voice my concerns to her. I also don't want to disappoint her since she has been looking forward to this visit for sometime. I no longer have the strength to support myself much less anyone else.

I have been allowed others to drain my energy reserves through my third chakra or will center. The will center is located in the solar plexus. Anatomically, this is where the liver is located as well as the stomach and the spleen. Elementally, the liver is an organ of fire. It is where we often store anger and rage causing migraine headaches, digestive disturbance, skin rashes and eye problems. My life force was being sucked out faster than I could possibly replenish it. Allowing this depletion of my life force certainly did not serve me or allow me to fully help others to heal. During deep meditation, I visualized a thick black hose attached to my third chakra draining my will, strength of self and my creativity. I was powerless to remove this cord due to the illness that had progressed within me. I asked other healers to remove the dark cord as it appears but my Angelic Guidance told them not to remove it yet, as it was not the proper time.

He seemed to understand as I attempted to explain my feelings although he was saddened and fearful of the future as was I. Our tears flowed together and mingled in a rare moment of closeness and shared pain. But I could feel myself falling out of control into the black hole of codependence. We held each other for a long time amidst assurances that our separation would only be for a short time. Our shared honesty brought us closer together and in the next few weeks we were kinder and more loving than we had been for a long while.

Thanksgiving dawns crisp and cold. As I rise to stuff the turkey and slip it into the oven, out in the yard under the old oak trees, foraged a flock of wild turkeys busily scratching up the last of the acorns. They looked like mourners in their black frocks. I wonder if they are here for the big domestic cousin who gave his life without choice for our feast this day or are they here to mourn for us. I surround them in Light and Love, and then give thanks as our bird goes to the oven.

Somehow the work always gets done and the day is successful and satisfying to all that share this day with us. This year of 1997 was to be the most memorable and deeply moving of any I could recall. As we thirty-one souls, stood in a large circle holding hands, each person recited what they were thankful for. I could barely contain my joy and gratitude as I looked into each face around that big circle. The children read stories, poems and blessings that they had written. They sang songs and hung their drawings and paintings created a few days earlier. This was our first Thanksgiving since my dad had passed over in August. The memories and the tears flowed readily as his spirit was strongly felt in our circle. One son-in-law eloquently expressed all of our feelings when he explained how grateful he was to stand in circle in that friendly old house at that moment in time and be part of our loving family.

Our family is a circle of strength and love
With each birth and every union the circle grows.
Every joy shared creates more love.
Every crisis faced together makes the circle stronger.

DECEMBER

I am beginning to awaken and remember who I am. This journey was necessary since I am a limitless being living in a limitless Universe. I am beginning to see through the veils of amnesia.

A sense of relief surrounds me since I made the decision to pull out of the Polarity Realization Institute's Registered Polarity Practitioner degree program. The R.P.P. program is the terminal degree in the practice of Polarity. It consists of 650 hours of study including hands-on practice. Polarity is a holistic health care program designed by Dr. Randolph Stone, D.O., D.C., D.N., over a sixty-year career. Polarity Therapy is one way of working with the fundamental energies of life, a way of bringing these energy currents to a state of balance by removing obstructions to their free flow throughout the human energy field. Establishing this state of flowing balance enables the life energies to bring about whatever healing needs to be done. This balanced condition is experienced as one of deep concentration and relaxation, as improved peace of mind, heightened awareness of one's fundamental nature and one's personal needs and potential. It incorporates a set of principles of energy flow, the Life Force, through pathways in the energetic and the physical body that directly nourish the endocrine glandular system, the organs and the nervous system.

The Polarity Therapist evaluates the ways in which an individual's energy flow is imbalanced, then using a variety of procedures assists the individual in establishing balance and harmony physically, emotionally and mentally. Diet and nutrition, stretching yoga postures, exercise, manipulation and the role of lifestyle and individual thought patterns are included in the rebalancing process.

The stress I felt was due to the driving and long absences from home rather than the classes. Most of the classes were interesting and challenging. Sitting with a group of energetic healers is uplifting and often a great deal of cleansing, healing work was accomplished by just being present. Now I miss my friends and colleagues. Behind me in the shadows of my consciousness lurks the word "failure". A strong sense of discontent surrounds me now. It is hard to settle into anything. I seem to be very distracted. I wish only to be where I can rest in the sunshine. I need to see green once more, to feel the sun on my face and shoulders, to let go of my protective armor and just relax.

I don't look back and I try not to acknowledge the presence of failure. As humans, we usually carry the unacknowledged, the unpleasant dark stuff on our backs. So much of our history is there sometimes threatening to bring us to our knees because of the load and accompanying pain it causes. We then develop a stiff neck so that we can't really rotate our heads to see our stuff but we feel the ever-increasing load. Our shoulders hurt, our backs ache, it is difficult to breathe deeply, we tend to slump and some of us develop humps from the congested energy. Polarity therapy is the only healing modality I know of that enables one to shed all the weight that has been shouldered for so long.

The only complaint I have about moving to North Carolina for the winter is the lack of Polarity therapists within three hours driving time. I usually receive distance-healing sessions each month while I am in the south. The results of distance healing are very similar except I find I miss the touch of the therapist's hands. In the case of distance healing, the healer and client are separated by geographic location only. The two energy systems are immediately brought together. The therapist consults with the client initially over the phone to determine what issues the client wishes to address in the session. Then the client either lies or sits quietly for about an hour while the therapist projects the clearing, repairs and balancing needed through intention focused on a quartz crystal. Pure quartz crystals carry the ability to magnify human thought forms many times through vibrational waves while conserving the energy level of the therapist. They are invaluable tools for anyone working in earth-based vibrational medicine.

Distance Polarity sessions combined with my own daily clearing and alignment enable me to stay balanced, aligned and able to work in the energy fields of others without absorbing their dark energies. Anyone working in energetic medicine learns early in their education how to protect themselves from the dark forces that exist in many forms, seen and unseen, everywhere around us. It is wise to have a teacher, mentor or guide when embarking on a path of healing others. Many over-zealous novice healers with big open hearts and no self-protection have fallen ill due to the parasitic energy forces they encounter while attempting to help others. I once questioned my teacher about vulnerability. She responded with a question. "What is the opposite of vulnerable?" When I answered the obvious, "invulnerable," she asked if that is the state I wished to be in. Of course, I said no, but asked how can I be open and vulnerable and still keep the boundaries of my own energy system clear. Once I had reached the place where I could define and describe who I wanted to be, I truly began to learn, gaining strength and integrity. It was about this time that I read Doug Boyd's book, *Rolling Thunder,* about a healer of the same name. I was deeply influenced by Rolling Thunder's life of healing and the reading had a deep and lasting effect on how I would maintain my integrity and focus in my work with others as a healer and medicine woman. Rolling Thunder always prayed and meditated on prospective clients for three days before he consented to work with them. I have adapted his policy to my own practice in addition to meditating on each client just before doing a session. I always ask for guidance from a centered introspective state and receive the information I need to help not only the client but also myself. This was my first big leap of faith. I was giving up control of situations and of outcomes, trusting in the Creator's all knowing.

As I drive to meet my daughter for a Christmas shopping trip, my mind travels back over the last five and a half years. I have felt so aware and energized, so eager to serve the will of God. It seems this comparatively short period of my life has been filled with more lessons and more teachers than before I was awakened and refreshed. I like the word refreshed rather than reborn because I felt at the time that I was washed clean of my ego-driven past. The fog in my mind was burned off by the glow of the pure white Light that now fills and surrounds me. I saw and felt the presence of my Guidance, the Angelic Realm. I heard their voices and I knew I was not alone nor had I ever been before.

I had been aware since early childhood of a presence around me. I saw shadows, colors and visions. Many times I witnessed miracles and heard faint voices but was too terrified to tell anyone as they might think me crazy or worse yet; they might think I was a religious fanatic. As I grew older, I persistently pushed that presence away so I could keep control of my life. As a child growing up in a fundamentalist religious atmosphere, we were taught that we were the children of God the Father and as such were watched and treated as children of our generation were treated by their fathers. Love existed somewhere out there in the outer reaches of space and time but punishment was sure to be swift and often cruel if we disobeyed the rules. If that was not enough of a deterrent to sinful behavior, then there was the threat of "The Big Book." I envisioned the dreaded book as having a page for each living being on earth. At the top of the page were all the pertinent facts about the individual and underneath that were three columns: Bad girl, good girl and total score. No wonder I "hit the street running," as my friend likes to say. I had no choice if I were to allow my spirit to grow in wisdom, truth and love, thereby preserving my soul. Every time I felt the presence of Guidance, I thought I could hear the teachings of my upbringing knocking on my door. I remembered the bigotry I witnessed as a child and I didn't want any part of that kind of religion.

Many times as I played with the horses in their stalls, grandma's hired man would hover nearby continually trying to fondle my budding breasts. I was ashamed and afraid as I scurried out of his reach. I told my mother but she said he just loved me so much that he wanted to hug me. Since he was a pillar of the church, she was sure he meant no harm. And then there was the smoking . . . .

I deeply loved and respected my grandmother. She was always there for me. She taught me and other youngsters that smoking, drinking and swearing were not acceptable in God's sight. One day when I was 8 or 9 years old, I ran up across the field to see my grandma. I eagerly looked for her around the house and barns. Then as I rounded the corner of the chicken house, I caught sight of her standing there, in the dusky light, smoking a cigarette. I tore out of there on shaky legs to hide in the hay mow for several hours contemplating what I had seen. My childhood innocence was being burned away. A wiser but more fearful girl emerged.

But yet, my belief in God or a Higher Power has never wavered throughout my life. I felt strongly connected to all that existed in nature but hovered outside of a strong bond with humanity. It wasn't until the spring of 1992 in Southern Pines, NC, that I would answer that persistent call. I had been feeling very empty and desolate, praying for guidance on how to proceed, where I fit in, what I could do to help others. I was feeling the need to give back. So much had been given to me over my life and I felt it was time to return my gifts to those in need.

I was riding regularly and very involved in dressage. I loved the discipline of the sport. There was spirituality about it, a truly grounded connection with the earth and her creatures. There was communication with the horse through subtle body language and the thought processes and through the energy field. Horse and rider moved as one being. I had a wonderful intuitive American Quarter Horse named Salt My Luck. He was always willing to give all he had to please me and in doing so, his muscles were often sore. I was drawn to an ad in one of my horse magazines for a school of equine massage in North Carolina. I felt this was something I could do to help my own horse and perhaps help other horses that suffered as mine did. I enrolled for a weeklong course taught by a truly gifted and loving being.

My class consisted of two other women, all of us with names beginning with "D", Dana, Diana and Deanna. There was something about this group that was exciting—nothing I could name at the time but I felt an energy surge whenever we were all together. I was invigorated and couldn't wait for my next encounter with them. I stayed in a ratty old motel downtown behind the Pizza Hut with my dog, Duffy. During the day Duffy went to a doggy day care nearby. One night after dinner as I was preparing to retire after giving Duffy one last walk, I heard running steps go by my window and then gun shots. Duffy and I hit the floor and I crawled to the bedside table and dialed the front desk.

I was advised to stay put that the police would take care of it. Doubt and fear did dampen my spirits a bit but the next day; I joked about my close encounter and let it go.

Our study began with human anatomy. Then we practiced on one another and finally progressed to hands-on touch with the horses in the area. I witnessed healing and a connection to the horses that I had never realized could exist between a human being and an animal. As my teacher would lay her hands on a horse, suddenly it would begin to moan and stretch. Sometimes it would go into a deep state of relaxation and bliss. Other times it would sweat profusely over the area she was touching. There was one horse, a thoroughbred that had been very resistant to being tacked up and ridden on the racetrack. A lovely, young animal with obvious potential but since he was unable to speak our language, he "spoke" through resistance. As we stood around the animal, my teacher worked his muscles deeply. He began to moan and groan softly at first but then let out a loud deep groan that seemed to come from deep in his gut. There was such a sense of relief. As he groaned, he stretched back with his front legs stiff and low while his rump was stuck in the air, much the way a dog stretches. We all stood back in awe at the sudden change in this noble lofty beast. Following the massage, he was saddled and taken out to the track and for the first time he went through the gate and ran without resistance or pain. I knew I was being shown something very special. My energy and enthusiasm continued to heighten.

Another day we were checking the temperature difference on the forelegs of another thoroughbred colt. We found the animal had one ice-cold leg and one very hot leg. My teacher asked that we all focus our attention deeply on this horse and ask for balance. We all placed our hands on his withers and stood in silence for a few moments. When rechecked, the horse's legs were of equal temperature. I witnessed these "miracles" in awe.

At the end of the week as part of our "graduation ceremony", we were given a treat. We were going to do group massages on each other. We each had our turn and then came to the last person in our group, Dana. Our teacher sat at her head, Diana at her feet and I stood at her hips. She was a diminutive woman with a reserved hardened look about her. She was a professional trucker and carried a chain wallet in her hip pocket. I had the feeling that life had worn hard on her psyche and that she had created this mask as protection from vulnerability and pain.

As our teacher began to work on the back of her head, the teacher's hands began to shake and quiver violently. There was a beautiful light surrounding all of us in the room. A sudden wave of the most incredible sadness hit me. It was as though someone had put a heavy dark sad blanket over us. I glanced at Diana and saw that the tears were rolling down her cheeks. We sat down near Dana and continued to sob uncontrollably. I felt the grief and the weeping of women throughout the ages. Meanwhile, Dana just lay there on the table as though in a deep sleep.

Never being one to show my emotions in public, I was shocked at the depth of the emotion that was pouring out of me in the presence of these women I had only met a few days earlier. What was happening here? Suddenly, there was a lifting of the weight of sadness and we ceased crying just as quickly as we had begun minutes before. We looked at one another with wonder and then at Dana, who at this time, sat up, stretched and asked what was wrong with all of us. We couldn't answer and just hugged one another, letting it go.

Later that evening, over dinner at a restaurant, we three students talked. Dana had changed since her massage that afternoon. She appeared lighter, smiled easily, had fixed her hair differently and was actually rather animated during our mealtime conversation. We asked questions that we hadn't dared ask before due to her closed demeanor. She eventually told us that years before she had witnessed the tragic death of her nine-year-old son. He had been hit by a car. She apparently had never grieved over her loss and had walled off that part of her life. It seems we had been allowed to be part of her long delayed grief process. We had been the facilitators of that much needed grief release. Little did I know at the time, that over the next few years I would be a facilitator for many more individuals who needed to release pent up emotions and trauma that will enable them to find health, peace and balance.

Having been through several graduations in my life, I can say this one stands out as the most life changing. I left there in a state of euphoria and disbelief, as though I had witnessed something in a dream. I was unable to put it all into perspective. My wonder and curiosity got the best of me and I called my teacher a few days after returning home to ask if I could return to speak with her about what I had experienced. She consented to see me on the following weekend. We sat together and talked for several hours. She told me that the release had taken place for Dana because the time was right and we had been chosen to assist. I told her of my visions and voices. She said I had been chosen to help others and that my mission would be revealed to me soon. She felt I was being carefully prepared for something specific. She said I should listen closely for guidance. I cried as she revealed these things to me because there was part of me who had known all of these things for a long while but had been resistant, pushing God away. I feared turning control of my life over to God. Every time this possibility came up in my conscious mind, I would say, "No, not now. Please let me be, I don't have time for this and I don't want to hear it." I wanted my life to stay exactly as it was. That is, of course, with all its isolation, anger, pain, suffering and loneliness. I don't know why I wanted it to stay the same. I guess there is comfort in the same old familiar pain. That old familiar pain and suffering is like a worn out pair of shoes that you won't give up even though they are destroying your feet. One who is born in a cage learns to love his cage. As a child, I had seen others who supposedly turned their lives over to Christ and "were born again". Many of them were dark, brooding, unhappy people who were zealots and bigots. That was not my idea of spiritual conversion. I loved life and was usually a happy joy-filled person. Life could be tough but I always found a way to be joyful no matter what. I left there with as many questions as answers. But there was a great sense of relief, a sense of permission, as if I had been battling many long years and had just received word the battle was over, there was no need to fight anymore, just accept the peace that was offered.

Only a few miles out of town on my way home, my tears forced me to pull off the road. I took Duffy out of the truck, tied him to a tree and stood in the presence of God and all creation, cleansed and baptized in faith and trust. A torrent of tears filled with energy, color and sound washed over me, washed away all of my past pain, loneliness and fear. I felt naked and scrubbed clean by the flood of my tears. I was filled with promise of the future and with pure joy. I have never experienced anything like the total surrender of my being to my God. I don't remember much of anything on that return trip. There was a sense of floating wonder. I do remember at one point, thinking, "How can I be driving and still not be aware of it?" There wasn't any fear, only a feeling of soaring. I began to journal this experience as soon as I arrived home.

What surprised me most at the receipt of this epiphany was how quickly I was transformed. I didn't appear to be any different than when I drove out there but inside, spiritually, I was newborn. Somehow others sensed my transformation. From that place of total surrender to the will of God, it seemed far less effort was required on my part to deal with the everyday challenges of my life. In bookstores, restaurants and shops, strangers would approach me with a smile and tell me their story that needed to be shared. I felt surrounded by light and joy, carried along, feet just barely touching the earth. I prayed frequently, opening my heart and mind with a receptivity I never thought possible. My mantra became "How may I serve?" Although I did not know how to meditate in '92, the answers came swiftly, telling me to use this time to study spiritual and religious texts as well as the metaphysical and the occult literature.

I was overflowing with enthusiasm and wanted to tell the world about my transformation. Quite naturally, those family members closest to me heard it first. I became an over-zealous missionary in my attempts to convert my family to my way of thinking until I realized my mission was better served by example rather than by preaching. The example of my life would be like a pebble dropped in a still pond. The ripples and their vibration would flow outward in ever-increasing circles touching and gently molding all they encountered.

As I learned to meditate from tapes and books, my inner resources began to open and broaden. I gained access to parts of self that I never knew existed. My husband, who had always previously been supportive of all my creative ventures was now, cautiously supportive throughout this process. In many ways, he was fearful as he witnessed the changes that were taking place very rapidly as I perceived my path in this life. What had served me before the transformation, no longer would serve or support me now. Nearly every evening, I fled to the sanctuary of my little studio upstairs to pray and meditate while the television belched out violence and ugliness downstairs. I wanted terribly to be an instrument of awakening and the more I gently tried to persuade him to open himself to God, the deeper he dug in his heels and resisted. The ice was forming on the lake of our marriage even back then.

As a former bank officer, I was accustomed to dressing in the appropriate attire for my position; suit, blouse, pantyhose and pumps. The image that persisted in my mind was of me standing there before all of creation in my best banking attire awaiting a job description. Each time I appeared dressed and ready to serve, I was told, "Go back, study and be patient." Three years of excruciating lessons in patience passed before I received that job description. The teachers appeared then too, one after the other. It was during this time that I discovered Polarity therapy. As Buddha said, "When the student is ready, the teachers will appear." Five years would pass before I was able to let go of all those conservative suits, finally giving them away.

It is raw and cold as my daughter and granddaughter plod along with me around the shops of Brandon searching for the right gifts for family and friends. It is dark as we return to our car and I realize how anxious I am to leave here for the south. There has been very little sunlight as is often the case in November and December in Vermont. I am after all, a creature of light. My skin is dry and stretched taut, my nose bleeds a little each morning from the dry air in the house. My eyes are bone dry and I am uncomfortable and discontented here in the damp cold. All is not well; all is not peaceful within. Even my car, after being washed, is soon covered with crud again.

I travel one last time to Ispwich to finish a make-up a class I missed the year before. The drive is excruciatingly painful and challenging. It does provide me the opportunity to say a few good-byes to some dear friends. I gratefully accepted a Polarity session from my soul sister and therapist, Nicky. The session is appropriately a "fiery" one since I had just attended a fire class. In Polarity we work with the elemental pathways of the body: Ether, air, fire, water and earth. Each pathway has a negative and a positive charge or polarity opposite as well as a neutral place. Each element nourishes and balances a different part of the body.

Ideally, all the elements exist as open pathways and flow in harmony along clear, aligned chakras and other energetic lines. Surrounding the body is the magnetic field known as the aura. The aura offers protection from negative forces upon our energetic system. Thinking of it as a giant multi-colored balloon around the body provides a helpful visualization. The aura consists of pulsating templates of many colors layered one over the other. Each template or layer extends further from the body and each supports a chakra that supports the endocrine and nervous system. Stored within the auric field is all the history of that being. The auric field tends to attract and accumulate toxins, negative energy, and mucus, light and color. Trauma and grief as well as all our relationships are stored in the aura. The aura is often full of holes if there has been alcohol or drug abuse. Surgical intervention in the body as well as anathesia will stay in the auric field until cleared. Numerous surgeries further deplete the aura giving the individual less protection. All sexual partners remain in the aura as small honing devices that drain our energy each time that particular partner thinks of us. A clean, vibrant auric field that is attuned to the Universal Life Force or higher vibrations will provide the individual with abundant life force and robust glowing health.

Working with the fire element is invigorating and energizing. Fire work turns on all the lights. It did not come as a surprise when, amidst a rush of tears, I suddenly found myself pouring out the tragic story of the burning of my grandmother's homestead.

New Year's Day, 1957, had been celebrated according to custom at Grandma's with the roasting of duck and all the traditional trimmings. I clearly remember the smells of the roasting duck, the wood smoke from the cook stove, the warmth and the love that had permeated the two-hundred-year-old rambling farmhouse. For me, going to Grandma's house, about a half a mile across the field from my own home, was as natural as going home. I had already spent much of my young life there in that secure nurturing fortress. I could not anticipate the fiery transformation that would catapult me from childhood to adulthood within the next twenty-four hours.

Throughout my childhood, my parents both worked out of town, so prior to school age, I stayed with Grandma and then, after I had started school, walked from the small one-room schoolhouse in the village up the long steep hill after dismissal each day. Other children who lived beyond Grandma's farm usually accompanied me. What adventures we found as we walked that mile or so. An intriguing waterfall that cascaded down over the slippery moss–covered rocks that called us to investigate during all seasons. We shared timelessness when we played and explored the waterfall. Only the voice of a parent calling from a slow-moving car on the dirt road nearby would rouse us from our fairy realm. More than once we were grounded for not coming straight home from school. Many times we went home with heavy hearts and a fair amount of fear for clothing torn by slipping and sliding on the icy rocks. Across the road from the waterfall, was a grove of sweet smelling white pine, grown close and comforting, capable of singing to our young ears. I often went into the pines when occasionally I was alone on my homeward journey where I would sit down sinking deeply in the pine straw safe from the outside world. This was the place where I felt a deep connection to all of creation and could feel as though I belonged. In times of deep sadness and disappointment, I entered that sacred place, threw myself on the ground spilling my tears into the earth where I always found comfort and clarity. A pattern was formed that would be with me for the rest of my life. There amidst the whispering pine voices, my vivid imagination would open like a lovely flower in the warm sunshine. I could be anyone, anything, be anywhere and do whatever I dreamed of. I was free, unfettered, unbound and I would soar like an eagle. I felt comforted by the spirits and guides that existed in the forest. Sometimes I lay down and breathed deeply of the mossy, sweet earthy smells emanating from my dear Earth Mother.

A short distance beyond the pine grove was a bubbling spring, a source of sweet flowing water bounded by rocks and old wooden rails. The dilapidated fence surrounding the spring was meant to keep the animals from falling in. This too, was a place of magic, of spirits and provided unending fascination for the mind of a child. I once discovered a golden frog in the spring. Each day I visited, picked up "Goldie" in my hands and talked with her. I carried her to school one day for show and tell. I carefully removed her from the jar I had prepared for her journey to school and slipped her back into her watery world. The next day I returned to find her belly up, dead. Through my guilt and sadness, I learned about leaving nature be in its natural state. Tough lessons for a young child.

As my homeward journey carried me higher up the hill, on the left stood the house. Architecturally, I guess it would be classified as a late eighteenth-century farmhouse. It was white, of course, two stories with a kitchen wing and an attached two-story woodshed. Just a few feet from the woodshed, was the outhouse, a place of fears but also a curiosity for my youthful spirit. Spiders and who knows what else lurked in the corners and rafters of the ancient seat of necessity. This was a place where it was required that you cover the toilet tissue with a large metal can to protect it from whatever it was that preyed on toilet tissue. There was a pail that contained corncobs, another containing lime and a scoop. A catalog was hung from a nail with a string around it to protect it from the beasts that scurried about. It was mysterious and frightening to a youngster and probably to a few adults as well.

This house did not have running water or central heating. It did have electrical wiring and a telephone, both quite primitive systems. Water was precious to us. It had to be gently and respectfully brought forth from the earth and then used sparingly. We learned respect and caution as well as humility in our attempts to obtain water. It was especially difficult to lure from the earth if a small person had been "messin" around with the outdoor pump. The handle of that old black pump had to be always left in the down position or the prime would be lost. Lost to where, I wondered. Where did it go, how far and how do we get it to come back? Grandma would sputter and feign anger as she went to the kitchen for a dipper of water to pour down the pump spout while vigorously pumping the handle. Sometimes the pump would take several trips to the kitchen for more priming water. I can see that house pump clearly even today. There was a strap to tie the handle down so that it could not be accidentally pulled up and left to lose its prime. There was always a bucket under the spout to catch any precious drips or drizzles. In addition to the well, rain barrels were strategically placed around the house under the gutters to catch rainwater for bathing and dishes. These barrels were particularly interesting to me because they became the habitat for many different critters. I never knew what I would find in those dark depths. It might be a small green frog, a snail, dragonflies or damselflies. Then there were the varicolored salamanders and newts. Occasionally, there would be a nearby box turtle or painted turtle lured by the water and the dampness surrounding the rain barrels. This home place, as my mother called it, was a fascinating place for a child to grow and learn.

The drinking water was contained in a pail on the old Hoosier cabinet with a towel over it for sanitation. The dipper lay next to it but one never ever drank from the dipper. It was to be used only to ladle water to a glass or other appropriate container. There did exist another well in the barn area. That pump was just as cantankerous as the kitchen pump. From the barn well, water was pumped into buckets and carried one in each hand, to the animals twice a day. A slow and arduous task on the best of days but a most difficult and physically demanding task on a cold winter day. The barn water was also used in the little shed called the milk house. The milk house contained a large tank that was filled with cold water and ice to cool the milk in the cans before it was bottled and sold. The method has long since disappeared with the pasteurization process. Never in my childhood did I ever think that this supply of water would not be sufficient to squelch the flames that would reduce my special place to ashes.

The milk house was the place where I sailed my first boat on my seventh birthday. My brother was born the day before and my gift was a beautiful red sailboat with a tall mast, deep keel and fluffy white sails. My younger sister and I stayed up at the farm with grandma while my father and oldest sister went to visit my mother and new brother at the birthing center. It was a lonely day for me and I was filled with many questions. Where was I to fit in now that my father had a real son rather than just a tomboy daughter? What would it be like to have a boy in our house of girls? Would I be expected to play with him like I was expected to play with my younger sister? My seventh birthday turned out to be a life-changing event for me as my relationship with my father changed rapidly in the next few months. I found I began to rely more on my grandmother's company, the animals I loved so much and the farm for the love and comfort I desperately craved.

I explored and romanticized every nook and cranny of the house and nearby sheds. There was the root cellar down in the bowels of the house. Dark, damp smelling and earthy, reached by a narrow stone lined passage from outside the house but also accessible by a secret passageway from a storeroom off the dining room. Runaway slaves, outlaws, women and children had all hidden down there from the many dangers that faced settlers of earlier times or so we imagined. The smell of the earth and stored vegetables in bins filled with sandy soil is what I remember most. The walls were lined with fruits, vegetables and meats all put up by the loving hands of my grandmother.

Now that I approach the age she was at that time, I marvel at all she created. Besides milking her cows, caring for the livestock, the horses and chickens, she fixed fences, delivered milk, harvested crops, taught Sunday school, read her Bible every day and was a claims adjuster for the local Farm Bureau Insurance Group. I remember riding with Grandma to inspect damage claims that occurred on sheep farms in the area. It was a cruel and gory sight to see the sheep and lambs with their backsides chewed out scattered around the field. Sometimes one or two would still be living but crying out in agony until the farmer put them out of their misery with a bullet to the brain. Now when I look back on those memories, I am surprised that I was allowed to tag along on those trips. Grandma had a very kind heart and she loved animals. She would keep an old cow even if it could hardly walk until she was forced to put it down. She knew the attack of the sheep by stray dog packs was terrible but it was part of being a sheep farmer in that part of the world. But when it came to doing necessary killings such as with chickens and hogs, she was very matter of fact. She seemed to be able to separate herself and step back from her heart to a logical place that held her emotions in check. Butchering a chicken or a hog to provide food for a family was also necessary and there was no room for emotions. My older sister and I would run and hide when Grandma brought a chicken to the block with her axe in hand. She matter-of-factly laid the chicken across the block and chopped off the head leaving the body to race around the yard headless spewing its lifeblood. It seemed no matter which way we ran, the headless chicken chased us. We were terrified.

On January 2, 1957, as we children returned to school under a cold overcast winter sky, my grandmother drove to the nearby city of Troy to complete some errands. High School for my sister and me was also located in Troy, New York, fifteen miles away. When the loudspeaker boomed out over my classroom calling me to the office, I knew something terrible had happened. My future husband Mac's face confirmed my fears as he told me that I was needed at home. Mac was a volunteer fire fighter. He was called from his work in a butcher shop and knew that my sister and I would want to be home. No one knew where my brother was. I didn't know it at the time but there was speculation that he was in the fire. The trip seemed to take forever although I know he drove as quickly as he could. As we approached the turn to Grandma's road, my eyes were filled with a vision of the huge flaming structure high on the top of the hill where the stately old house had always stood.

I bolted from the car halfway up the hill and ran the rest of the way as though I could somehow make a difference. It was an inferno at that point. I stood alone in shock, grief and horror as the fire consumed and transformed all that was there including me. Just as we are born alone, naked and cold, we need to go through our transformations alone. A kind of rebirth, a time of trial, a stripping away of the dross to reveal the pure magnificent gold that is hidden and unseen by our veiled eyes. I was like molten metal, soft and receptive, trembling in my weakness yet already cooling and taking the shape of my aloneness, the shape of my growth. No longer a child, I had put away my childish ways, actually they had been burned away. I was now being prepared to step away and sever those strong ties of the farm and family. I watched with the open eyes and heart of a child as high in the crumbling rafters for just an instant I felt my soul connect with the blackened figure of Grandma's cousin, Viola, as she was revealed clutching her little dog before she fell into the fiery depths of what was used to be the house. Two aged women died there, one who was blind named Bertha, the other Viola, as well as a dozen cats and two dogs. In the following days, Grandma and I would retrieve and pile in the wheelbarrow the bodies of our four-legged friends. I dug the graves out behind the corn crib as she gently buried each one. Then we would attend the funerals for the two human beings who had been our friends and our family.

That night, safe in my father's house with my grandmother kneeling beside me, we prayed. We were side by side, each in her own grief but somehow sharing. Today she continues to guide my life from the other side as she has in many previous lives. We slept very little that night or for many nights after. I felt such a sense of emptiness and aloneness, a feeling that would be with me for the rest of my life. The sight of that figure in the rafters would haunt me until a day in 1997 when I poured out my story to Nicky, my therapist.

In 1995, I received a flyer from a friend, describing a weekend meeting in Boston, called Body and Soul. Many of the presenters were well-known authors whose work I had just studied. I was drawn to attend. I felt this was an opportunity for my husband and me to get away for a weekend that would be beneficial to both of us. He declined but said I should go ahead. I began to scour around to find a companion who would share driving and expenses. At the last minute, my friend decided not to go and I found myself alone on the road to Boston. I would not allow my ego-self to think about what I was doing because then my fears would push out all rational thought. It became a lesson in trust, allowing myself to be powerless. I do believe we have two emotions that control everything, our speech and our actions. They are love and fear. Our e.g.o. will "edge God out" as soon as we allow fear to enter our minds.

I prayed fervently throughout the entire four-hour drive for courage and safety. I had never taken a trip like this alone before into a big city. However, the trip was effortless and before I knew it, I was opening the car in an ominous concrete parking garage maze beneath my hotel. There out of the semi-darkness appeared a dark man in uniform who asked very politely if he could help me. I accepted and we were on our way to the elevator and the registration desk in minutes.

I stood in my room in the lengthening shadows of that Friday afternoon feeling like I had ridden in on a magic carpet. After a brief prayer of thanksgiving, I went down to the bus that was to take us to the World Trade Center to hear the opening keynote speaker who just happened to be Maya Angelou. I was one of the first people on the bus and sat right behind the driver. The bus began to fill when suddenly my eyes met the eyes of a beautiful woman in white. She greeted me politely and asked if she could sit next to me. She told me her name and said that she had been sent by Higher Guidance to see me. She came to provide answers to many questions I had been pondering for sometime. She was to bring me a message of hope, love and grace. I was dizzy with astonishment and joy. We spent the next two days together, me asking questions, she teaching. Two others would join us the next day. Long lasting bonds of friendship and love were formed that weekend.

My system opened and expanded like a beautiful lotus flower. As an artist, I could never quite capture the beauty of a spectacular sunrise. The tools we have are just not sufficient. Now my words cannot adequately describe the rapturous feelings of my heart during that weekend and a lengthy period afterward. My new teacher explained to me gently that I needed to enjoy the time of instruction and rest, as a time would come soon enough when I would wish for a time out from service. It was with wet eyes and a soaring, grateful heart that I drove out of Boston on Sunday at sunset in a heavy downpour. A double rainbow appeared, God's gift of the promise of more to come. A sign that I was to become involved in building the rainbow bridge between people of differing colors.

The following day as I walked the sidewalks in Rutland plugged into my headphones listening to the Paul Winter Earth Mass; I received my long-awaited job description. A loud clear voice came in over the blare of the music and brought me, shaking and crying, to my knees. I was covered with "spirit bumps" from head to toe as I heard the voice declare, "You are to teach, you are to write and you are to sing." Somehow I made my way home where my eldest daughter appeared. She asked if I was OK. I was white and shaken. I told her what had just happened. She looked rather dubious and soon left. I prayed for clarification; teach what? Writing was easier as I was already journaling daily but singing? "Oh Lord, I cried, I can't sing." A softer gentler voice responded telling me to teach people how to live in the next century; find my voice and sing out for what I believed in.

Now it is 1997; Winter Solstice and Christmas are almost upon us. My dad always sent me off on my various sailing adventures with sound and loving advice, "Deanna, keep your feet dry." Well, lots of water has passed under my keel; so far my feet have remained dry.

Our family Christmas celebration is far different from Thanksgiving. Those of us who are able to do so try to get together at one house but more often than not, we are separated. My husband and I generally travel from house to house allowing the children to stay put. This year is not like the past Christmases as we are able to join one another at our daughter's house in Poultney. We all participate in a hilarious gift-giving game called Chinese Auction. We have enjoyed playing this game for several years. It begins with one person picking a gift from the stash that we have all brought. The next person up can take the gift the first person picked or pick another from the pile and so it goes until the end when the last person gets to choose any gift he/she wants from all that have been opened. It provides for interesting family dynamics. We all gather together at the table for a meal of sausage, peppers and home fried potatoes prepared by my husband. The joy feels more exquisite to me than I recall feeling before. We will learn later it will be the last time we share together as a family in this house. This house will be sold and my daughter and her family would move to Virginia in the following year.

Many times in the past ten years, we had been welcomed as a family group in another daughter's home. Their home is now, at Christmas, a place of discontent and of great sadness. It is a feeling that seems to permeate all that enter. I find it increasingly challenging to visit what was once a warm and loving home. I realize that none of these changes are in my power to control and as my eyes continue to be too painful to use, I am too weary to even attempt to do anything except try to heal myself. The coming winter will mark the breakup of that marriage and one home will become two. There are superstitious people who believe ill fortune will come in a group of three incidents. In our case, two huge changes are already in motion. I watch the play of energy back and forth amongst my family members. It is tide-like, a wind tide—where there is shallow water it will flow to another shore to rise high and powerful while it cleanses and oxygenates all life in the area. Then as the wind drops or changes directions, the water will return again to the original shore to do likewise. Our relationships fluctuate as the tide with the powerful winds of the four directions. As with all tides, be it moon or wind; the source is the instigator, the power, and the original spark of perpetual motion, the Breath of Life.

I had a healing dream just before we left for North Carolina near the end of December. I have to go up Grandma's hill with my car. There is lots of snow on the road. I try to go up but cannot make it so I back down to get a running start. As I reach the bottom of the hill, another car zooms in and squeezes in ahead of me. Suddenly there is another car that moves in behind me. We all give the hill a go but the first car in line cannot make it and we must all back down again. Finally, I push the other two cars up the hill to the top. A door appears. I tell the young woman with me not to open the door because it is winter but she doesn't listen and opens the door anyway. It takes all the strength we both have to close that door once again against the furious cold wind and blowing snow.

December 26, my husband Joe, my dog Duffy, elderly cat Pumpkin and I leave Vermont to pick up my mother in New York State for the trip. When we arrive, Mom is not packed. She has forgotten what day she was to leave. I hurriedly pick out a few pieces of clothing and her personal articles load them in her old brown cardboard suitcase and we are on the road south. Mom insists on sitting in the back seat with the pets. Pumpkin the cat has already resigned himself to the travel crate leaving Duffy to switch laps between Mom and me for the entire trip. My husband, Joe, prefers to drive straight through for the 800-mile trip. It takes approximately sixteen hours because of the added stops for the pets. We make regular stops to eat in restaurants rather than in the car so the miles and the hours go by quite quickly until the last three hours. That is always the worst part of the drive. I find I cannot drive at all and must keep my eyes tightly closed most of the time to find any relief from the pain and gritty feeling. My husband is a man with a mission to deliver all of us to our destiny and we make it without incident.

For many years, I have not lived with my mother for over a week at a time. This month-long visit will surely raise all kinds of questions and challenges for both of us. I look forward to a time of insight into our relationship. There have always been major differences between us as well as some basic trust issues that occurred during my childhood that need to be resolved. Now in her advanced years, I may finally find understanding and the gift of peace with my mother that will benefit both of us.

A few days later, Joe flies back to Vermont. Sadly, his restlessness has never allowed him to stay for very long in this peaceful place. My dream the night before he left brought a feeling of dread into my heart. For some reason, he had to drive up a tree, a tall, snow-covered tree then turn around and come back down. He did it once successfully, and then he attempted to do it again. I stood on a hillside watching. He backed around and I was suddenly filled with fear. He might slip and fall to the bottom. I saw the car coming towards the tree. It appeared to be going too fast. Then it wasn't a car any longer but a Jeep Cherokee. He climbed to the top and then it just fell out of the tree. I could see him sitting in there, one arm across the back of the seat. I watched as one hand brushed his nose. Our eyes met as he glanced over at me. I saw the look of sadness and resignation on his face as the Jeep hit the ground and exploded. The nagging dread stayed with me for several days but then the cleansing feeling of relief and freedom brought on by being home in the south pushed the memory of the dream away. At last I am home.

I came to love You late,
O Beauty so ancient and so new;
I came to love You late.
You were within me and I was outside,
Where I rushed about
Wildly searching for you like some
Monster loose in your beautiful world.
You were with me but I was not with you.
You called me, You shouted to me,
You broke past my deafness.
You bathed me in Your Light,
You wrapped me in Your Splendor,
You sent my blindness reeling.
You gave out such a delightful fragrance,
And I drew it in and came breathing
Hard after You.
I tasted, and it made me hunger and thirst;
You touched me and I burned to know
Your peace.
CONFESSIONS OF AUGUSTINE, BY ST. AUGUSTINE

JANUARY

"It was on fire when I lay down on it"
ROBERT FULGHUM, TITLE OF BOOK

S unrises in my home in the south are spectacular spiritual experiences of rebirth and resurrection. The house itself is built high upon pilings because of the possibility of high water from time to time. The land has been shaped by the flow of Broad Creek and forms a soft arrow point. The house is designed to compliment that arrow shape and takes advantage of water views from every window in all directions. In front flows Broad Creek, a wide tea-colored estuary of the mighty Neuse River and Pamlico Sound. Marshes, fertile nurseries for developing shellfish, lie on two sides of the house. The other side or drive side faces a long span of woodland with the white steeple of the Baptist church in the distance. Sunrises and sunsets are special times on my deck. Stargazing and moonlight romanticizing are also magical. From the comfort of my bed, I just need to open my eyes and sit up to see the first fiery glow in the eastern sky out over the Gulf Stream. I call this daily event, the Glory Glow. I sit in awe as I am privileged to witness once again the transformation from darkness to light. The colors are soft but vibrant and not reproducible even by the finest artist's palette. The clouds in the east sometimes give the illusion of high mountain peaks. I offer thanks for the opportunity to return once more to the house, to the Light.

According to Native American teachings I have studied, the east is the place of the ancestral Spirit Keeper, Wabun. This is the place where we sow the new seeds for our next harvest. It is where we begin the cycle of life again. Each day we are given a chance to do it again, to be reborn in the fresh new Light of our Creator. It is a place of youth, playfulness and joy, of healing and where we honor the element of air. Our Father Sun rises here as well as our Sister Moon. As I wrote earlier, the majestic eagle is symbolic of the winds of the east. As we proceed to the south, we honor Shawnodese, Spirit Keeper of the south. Here we find the place of summer, of passion, bloom, relationship, prosperity and abundance. Water is the element of the south bringing about our creativity and the flow of the feminine aspect. Coyote is the animal related to Shawnodese. He teaches us to laugh at ourselves and the futility of chasing our own tails. I have written of the direction of the west so will just mention that Mudjekeewis is the Spirit Keeper, the Grizzly Bear the animal associated with the west and the element is fire. In the north, we find the Spirit Keeper, Waboose. This is the place of winter, of coolness, healing, preparation, wisdom and the integration of all we have previously learned into the element of Earth. The north is represented by the White Buffalo Calf who brought the legend of the pipe and the sacred herb, tobacco to the Native Americans.

Sometimes I am suddenly awakened by some signal and there is the Glory Glow. I bathe in the beauty of it for about five minutes and then it is gone, the sky neutral once more. It is as though I have been given my own glimpse of God's promise of another chance to try again as it is when we see a rainbow.

January in this part of North Carolina can be quite blustery and cold but it may also be just the opposite, balmy and wet. No matter which, the sun usually shines through bringing the life force in abundance. My mother takes to the mild southern winter like a duck takes to water. She goes out walking each day, slowly at first and then as her strength and endurance build, she increases her speed and distance. Within two weeks, she is carrying armloads of wood upstairs to the wood box by the stove. I am amazed to watch the ability of her eighty-five year old heart and lungs to recover the strength of a younger person. She likes to attend church so each Sunday we motor over to the little white

Baptist church here in our rural village. After church, we drive into the nearby town of Oriental to eat a sumptuous southern-style buffet dinner. It becomes quite clear early on that Sunday is the day I will devote entirely to my mother's wishes. It feels good to give to her and I deceive myself into thinking I am recovering from the fatigue and dry eye condition.

I visit a couple of physicians in New Bern to see if they might have a different approach to the dryness and the inability to keep my eyes open. It is with no small measure of shock, that I receive their diagnosis of Sjogrens Syndrome.

Sjogrens is an autoimmune disease in the family with lupus, chronic fatigue syndrome and multiple sclerosis. My friends and I go online to attempt to find out more about this disease we have never heard of. I seem to be a classic case and it is recommended that I see a rheumatologist at Duke Medical Center. The more I research this disease, the more saddened and frightened I become. There is no known cure and as it is systemic, various organs of the body could become affected. Fatigue and joint pain as well as digestive issues and tooth decay become part of my life. I sign up for the newsletter and support group called Moisture Seekers. The letters from Sjogrens sufferers initially bring out much compassion but deep inside me they are a source of increased pain and fear. Not many people including doctors seem to have ever heard of this quite common disease that is more apt to strike women, especially after menopause. I felt that perhaps I had developed this disease so that I could bring attention to Sjogrens as well as teach others about it. Many women have gone undiagnosed for years because of the many and varied symptoms and lack of knowledge in the medical community. Various symptoms such as joint pain, mouth dryness, dental carries, liver or abdominal pain, fatigue, depression and dry eye often lead a patient to many different physicians. If the disease was brought out into the public and professional community then perhaps the sufferers would find solace and hope as modern medicine evolves.

An insidious feeling of hopelessness and a need to sleep has begun to invade my very being. I am not sharing these feelings with my mother. She doesn't seem to understand what is happening to me and I don't want to worry her. She lost one daughter, my older sister,

Marilyn to cancer at the age of thirty-seven in 1974. As it is, she often wrings her hands and questions no one in particular as to the origin of my blindness. She emphasizes that we haven't had anything like this previously in our family. She finds some comfort in the belief that our family diseases are genetic or accidentally caused by the diseased person. That way there is someone to blame for the whole thing.

My depression deepens as my husband's phone calls became more infrequent. I find my mother grating on my nerves. My anger flares up at her quite suddenly over silly inconsequential things. I am preparing all our meals. She is unable to assemble her thoughts clearly enough to make a sandwich. She has to ask me at each meal where the dishes are so she can set the table. I knew her memory was failing but I didn't realize to what extent she had progressed. She sits in front of the TV all evening sleeping and then complains she is unable to sleep all night in bed. I am tired and my patience is growing thinner by the day. She is scheduled to return north in early February but as the date nears she has decided she would like to stay longer. I cannot bring myself to send her back to the cold weather so her return is postponed.

I initially asked my husband to come down and fly back with Mom the first part of February. Even though she has decided to stay another month, he is coming as planned. I am anxious and eager to see him after nearly three weeks of separation. Now I think I understand why I have been fatigued for months. Surely he will be compassionate since I have what appears to be a debilitating disease that may severely limit my active participation in the remainder of my life. If ever I needed my partner, it is now. Isn't this what the vow of marriage is all about? In sickness and in health, we promise to love, honor and support one another now and in the future. These words have a hollow ring to them.

It is increasingly challenging for me to read so I spend a great deal of time lying down in meditation. Consequently, I am practicing lucid dreaming, writing down all the details in what has become my unrecognizable scrawl. I repeatedly ask to be given that which would help me see. Yogananda's prayer comes to mind:

Remove the veil between us; come, Spirit, come!
I yearn to know Thee and to hear Thy voice.
When I pray to Thee, I want to realize that Thou art listening.
Show me the way to reach Thee!

I recall a few years ago when my mother was hospitalized for vascular surgery in the early spring. The surgery itself went well but within a few hours the graft in her vein had pulled apart and she hemorrhaged heavily. I stayed with her for twenty-four hours, sleeping in a chair near her bed. Needless to say, I slept little. By noon the following day, my sister came to relieve me at Mom's bedside and I left for the drive to my parents' home to rest before tackling the remaining drive to Vermont where I was living at that time. The twenty-minute drive to my rest stopover was difficult because of my fatigue. I fought sleep and double vision for the entire trip. I reached their house, fell into the bed only to find the noise of the traffic on the busy nearby highway upsetting. I was accustomed to quiet natural sounds of the woods at my home. I lay there trying to rest but became more agitated thinking I could be home in the time spent lying there wide-eyed. I got up, made coffee and left. Fifteen minutes later, I couldn't keep my eyes open. I was near the old cemetery where both my grandmothers and several other relatives are buried. I have always found comfort in this cemetery because as a child I came here regularly with my grandmother, mother and father to mow the grass. We usually spread a blanket on the ground and shared a picnic lunch. I have many pleasant childhood memories about investigating the secret places of the cemetery with my sisters. We children would play amongst the stones while the adults performed their maintenance chores. It was a place of contentment and quiet for me. I didn't know much of sadness back then. I now find myself making the turn and driving the short distance to the cemetery where I knew I could safely pull off the road and take a nap. The sun was very warm, the birds were singing as I climbed out of my pickup to say a quick prayer at Grandma's gravesite. I prayed for my mother's recovery. I prayed for the energy and stamina to allow me to return home safely. I don't know how long I stood there and prayed. I know I went to a deep meditative place within me. When, at last I opened my eyes, the world around me was different. The area seemed to be bathed in rich golden light. I felt energized and filled with light. I got back in my truck, opened the Bible I always carried with me and the following passage leaped to my eyes: "You chart the path ahead of me and tell me where to stop and rest. Every moment you know where I am. You know what I am going to say before I ever say it. You both precede and follow me and place your hand of blessing on my head." Psalms 139: 1-5

I cried out in joy. Never before had I felt so alive and sure. I drove out the old iron gates and headed north to Vermont. The ride was beautiful, and made even lovelier by the huge patches of wild lupine blooming by the roadside and bathed in that same bright golden light that had surrounded me in the cemetery. I felt compelled to write a song and began humming it as I drove. The words were, "Come with me, Mama, before they cut the wild flowers; come with me, come and see what the Lord has created for you, Mama. This is your day. Come with me, come and see before they cut the wild flowers."

The road narrowed shortly after the stretch of lupine. Up ahead I saw the flashing lights of emergency vehicles. I slowed to a crawl as I passed a horribly crushed car and truck in a macabre embrace. This is upsetting for most drivers, I think, and I was no exception. I said a silent prayer for the victims followed by a prayer of thanksgiving for my own safety. When I arrived home, I was still wide-awake and filled with energy. I attempted to tell my husband what had happened to me but somehow it didn't seem so spectacular in the telling. As I lay down to sleep, the vision of that golden glow was still fresh in my mind. The next day, upon reflection on the previous day's experience, it hit me—had I not stopped at the cemetery for a time, I might have been struck by the drunken young man in the stolen car who smashed into the innocent truck driver, killing both. As I made my way back down the road to the hospital the following day, I could not find any trace of the lupine that had inspired me the day before.

I find in these last days of January that I am driving less and less. I still struggle to take Mom to church and out to lunch on Sundays but that is about it. As the day of my husband's arrival approaches, I decide I cannot make it to the airport, so I call a friend to drive me the twenty-seven miles to pick him up. My anxiety level has increased as the reality of his visit nears. We have so much to speak of. It is no longer just the icy patches in our marriage. Now it is the sickness in my body as well. I realize how much I need him now more than ever before. The strong independent woman has become blind and frail. I have always held the attitude that whatever might befall me, I would figure out a way to take care of myself financially and emotionally. That illusion is fast blowing out with the fog but the flood tide is coming in.

> *O my soul, why be so gloomy and discouraged?*
> *Trust in God—my God! O my soul.*
> *I shall again praise Him for His wondrous help.*
> *He will make me smile again,*
> *for He is my God!*
>
> PSALMS 43: 5

FEBRUARY

*The longing of the human heart to be loved for itself
is a something caught from the Great Divine Heart.*
GOD CALLING, EDITED BY A.J.RUSSELL

I am acutely aware of my heart pounding in my chest and throat as I hear the plane land and taxi up to the disembarking area. I step back in a group of people and watch for the first glimpse of my husband coming through the door. Suddenly there he is looking very somber and gloomy. We hug as he scowls at me, and then appears to cheer up as he hugs my friend. My expectations sink once again and the old familiar feeling of dread covers me like a heavy black cloak. My eyes are tightly shut most of the time so I gladly accept the hand of my friend as we walk to the car and then to the restaurant for lunch. My husband seems quite uncomfortable with my near blind state.

A passage from *God Calling* comes to mind: "When human support or material help of any kind is removed, then my power can become operative. I cannot teach a man to walk who is trusting to a crutch."

Truth has always resonated through me with cunning assurance, an inner knowing that it was so. But on the other hand, fiction haunts me like a prowler, nagging on and on until at last I get a sense of the wrongness of it and am able to put the pieces together. One of those times was during my husband's visit.

The first conversation we shared after we were alone consisted of his question, "Have you made any decision yet about our marriage. What do you have in mind? How do you see our future together?" All fair questions, although seemingly insistent and inappropriate given the state of my health and the fact that we haven't been together in over a month. When I left after Christmas, I had hoped to give some serious thought to the state of our relationship and come up with some kind of plan. But then I became preoccupied with my illness and had put him off for an answer on the marriage dilemma. Now here he was, as he said, "having been on pins and needles for some time," asking me what my decision was. I mumbled that I had not had much time to think about our marriage. He said, "You can see we are not good for each other. In fact, it seems we bring harm to each other." I admit that sometimes that seems to be true. We continue to talk for quite some time and then sleep fitfully for the remainder of the night.

The following night as we climb into bed together, he reaches for me. Initially, I stiffen but then I yield to his embrace determined to try once more. Maybe this is a likely place to find some thread to cling to. Suddenly, a voice booms in my head saying, "This is not what your life is all about. You deserve more than this." Tears flow so readily as I quickly pull away and escape to the bathroom. By the time I am able to return and he asks what is wrong, I am once again composed and I tell him I just don't feel like being intimate.

The next night, I retire early with many questions to ponder. I sense dishonesty in him throughout the day. I heard him come out of the study and head out towards the kitchen. My intuition tells me to follow him. As I round the corner of the kitchen, I realize he is in my studio on the portable phone with the door shut. I explode in anger. Of course, he is able to excuse and explain any of his behavior. He turns it around and makes it sound like it is all about me. We, once again, talk late into the night. I strongly sense the presence of another woman as I have so many times during our marriage. My intuition, keenly developed from my energy training, is on to the bits of truth cleverly hidden behind the veils of dishonesty.

The remainder of our time together is spent congenially working side by side in the house and out in the yard. No decisions are made about the future of our relationship. There is a perfunctory goodbye and he is gone. Relief sets in but something nags away at me.

A couple of days before my husband is to leave, a call from the real estate broker in Vermont who had been trying to sell the farmhouse we had been renting, shocks both of us. He has called to inform us that he has a contract and we would need to be out of the house by May. We are very surprised for we felt it would take some time for the house to sell because of the rather high asking price. Actually, the prospective buyers have made a lower offer and they are successful in negotiating a lower price with the seller. We hastily decide to fix up one of the apartments in my husband's office building where we can live until something else comes along or until he retires to North Carolina. I am grateful for the time spent in that old farmhouse. It has been a joyous and comfortable home for our family. Now apparently, it is time to move on. I am not fearful about moving because I am so content here in our North Carolina home. I wonder what this says about our relationship issues. We will have to wait until the rebirth of a new spring to appear on the horizon of our lives to see where this chapter takes us. The mystery of a new moment, a new day, and a new year awaits us. It is sad to think of moving out of the old house which reminded me of my childhood. All the other times we have moved our home, I have been there to take charge and to pack. Now, because of my illness, my husband is going to have to do it himself. He assures me that he will manage quite well. He will take care of setting up the apartment for my return in the spring. In actuality, many of my things were dumped in a storage shed. I was given access to it that summer and was deeply distressed at what I found.

After he leaves, when I awake the following morning, a waning moon and a brilliant Venus greet me. Their reflection on the creek is an impressive sight as I believe it will be another twelve years before we see them positioned in such a pattern again. The little plants and flowers are all beginning to show signs of blooming. The buds are there ready to burst forth. My hibiscus that has wintered in the house is all budded out. So it is near, that wonderful sometimes elusive but always welcome spring rebirth and renewal.

I pray that God will teach me to cleanse quickly and thoroughly of all my old outdated thought forms and karma. "Please", I continue,

"Let me make a difference. Let me help as many people as possible in whatever time I have left here."

The last gift I am to receive from my husband is a kayak. It was being built by one of our talented local wooden boat builders. Unfortunately, it is not quite finished yet. But I note many mornings at dawn when I could truly be one with the watery presence of Earth Mother, the feminine creative flow. I could become part of it and perhaps find my true self in its dark mysterious depths. How I long for the rich velvety softness, the salinity, the slight odor of brackish water. I long to be reborn once again—reborn in our Great Mother even if her waters are compromised. I vividly recall my baptism two years ago. The time has come to flow with her in harmonious joining.

My re-baptizing took place in June of 1995 in the creek directly in front of my home. At five in the afternoon in a light rain, the local preacher and I walked slowly hand in hand out into the creek until we were waist deep in the warm brown water. A few neighbors stood by on the shore singing, "As We Gather by the River". The experience was life changing, as it should be. I will never forget the taste or the delicious feel of the salty water as the preacher tipped me over backwards and dunked me under. It all seemed to happen in slow motion and remains very clear to me. As I surfaced, the light was brilliant and seemed to be all around us. It was as though the clouds had parted and the Light of God shown down on me. I felt the presence of God everywhere. A great peace descended on me and I was aglow with joy. The rain had stopped and the small group standing on the shore were singing, "Blest Be The Tie That Binds", as the preacher guided me back. Everyone came forward to help me up the stony bank, hugging and blessing me as I was passed from one to the other—everyone except my husband that is! His sadness and fear struck me like a blow to my heart as our eyes met. He stood half-hidden beneath an umbrella back from the group. To me, his cold eyes were somehow judging me. I felt no warmth, no love, only disdain from him. I felt a coldness, a distance and a lot of fear from him that day and I realized the depth of resentment he felt for me.

In the early morning we had sat together in the little church across the way listening to the preacher tell us that the Lord had prompted him to write a new sermon during the night. This new sermon was to be for one in the congregation who desperately needed the message. I prayed throughout the service that my husband would receive the message that I was certain was given for him to hear. The preacher urged whoever received the message in their heart to come forward and kneel with him on the altar. My husband did not approach the altar. After we returned home, he made fun of the sermon. I remember the preacher saying one time that the strongest are the most difficult to get through to. He said God knows and will not give up. God will win the battle. My husband is running hard; he is hiding behind his personal shield. After the well-wishers left, we talked about his feelings and behavior. The miracle of the Light during the baptism was shocking and brought about fear. Many people have the same reaction when faced with pure energy and Light. But for me, I had been cleansed, reborn and recommitted to serve God that day in the creek..

The initial glow of the day faded and now I feel like straw, dry and brittle, ready to burn up in a quick flash of anger. Perhaps there will be nothing left but a tiny dusting of ashes which will blow away in the wind to be forgotten. T.S.Eliot wrote in his poem, *The Hollow Men:*

> We are the hollow men,
> we are the stuffed men leaning together,
> headpiece filled with straw, Alas!

I am reaching out now which is difficult for me to do. It is so painful for me to ask for help from neighbors and friends. Receiving loving-kindness and caring is uncomfortable for me. I am letting down those barriers of fear, shedding my armor. I feel frail. I am human therefore I hurt, I bleed and I die a little each day.

Self-recrimination fills me because my suffering has not been like so many I have witnessed around me. I have not suffered physical pain that is unbearable. I have not suffered degradation. My suffering is more on an emotional and spiritual level. I thank God for that. I know this is a gift to be cherished once I get beyond the wrapping. I must keep reminding myself of that fact. I must cleanse and shed my old ways, my old fears. However, I am afraid. I am frustrated and angry. I reach out to friends and healers hoping someone can help me. I cannot seem to help myself anymore. There are days when I want this life to end. I want so much to leave this life and return home to God. The very same feelings and remembrances I had as a newborn infant struggling to breathe through fear and fluid-filled lungs.

My nervous system is fragile at this point. Making the decision to pull out of the Polarity Institute when I did was a wise move. I still have to finish the Anatomy and Physiology course and the exam. I am attempting to study a little each day but it is very stressful. I feel like I have been pushed to this point by an unseen force that will enable me to truly cleanse, to listen and to grow in spirit and wisdom. This is the dark side of my soul revisited, another opportunity for expansion after a lengthy time of contraction. Contraction always equals expansion. Venus is still influencing our lives with her beauty and light. The moon is in Pisces now, a new moon that will allow for expansion. God, may I allow the impressionable poet to express herself.

In the Gospel of St. Thomas, Jesus says, "There is within you that which will redeem you if you bring it forth, or destroy you if you do not bring it forth. If you run from anguish, if you don't meet it, you will live a life of anguish; but if you are willing to dive into it and bring it forth, you will be liberated in truth." Jesus also said, "If you know how to suffer, you do not suffer; if you know how to die, you do not die. That is what I am continually pointing to when I say: Meet your greatest fear. Meet your emotions. Meet your anguish. Meet your karma. Don't do battle with your emotions, just meet them. Karma cannot survive this meeting."

I hear less and less from my husband since he returned north. Mom doesn't ask any questions so we don't talk about it. I recall a dream; my husband had taken me to court. I was accused of being me. Because of that fact, I was unfit to be his wife. The judge asked my husband a list of questions: Does she drink or smoke? Does she commit adultery? Is she an unfit mother? Is she unclean? Is she sexually incompatible? And so on. My husband kept saying, "No" to each question. Finally, the judge asked him, "But why then are you here?"

The eye doctors have suggested inserting puncta plugs in the tear ducts of my eyes hoping to save what little tears I am making and keep them in my eyes a bit longer. They are tiny silicone plugs that fit snugly in the tear ducts at the corners of the eyes. They can be inserted in the top and bottom ducts or just the bottom, which is what I consented to. I am able to retain the plugs for about three weeks. Finally, the itching and pain are so intense, I have them removed. At this point my eyes are so dry I am using a case of artificial tears a month. I cannot be without a small vial of tears for over a minute. Nights are the most difficult as my eyes dry out so much that when I rouse up, I am unable to open them due to the intense pain. As I climb into bed, I insert the artificial tears and then top it off with a heavy coating of eye ointment that is the consistency of petroleum jelly, over both lids. This coating seals the moisture in for a much longer period of time. I am still getting up two or three times a night to treat my eyes but at least not every hour as was the case. Periodically, an infection called Blepharitis develops in the lids of my eyes from the invasion of impurities that cannot be cleansed by the natural flow of tears.

My neighbors continue to offer Mom rides to church and take her to concerts and plays. Meanwhile, I am having difficulty cooking for us. One more creative activity I have enjoyed is being taken from me. I am angry and despondent much of the time. I am desperate to find someone to fly back with my mother the first week in March. As this lesson in detachment continues, I hold onto the illusion that I can heal myself if I am left alone. My husband comes through for me by purchasing tickets for my daughter and her three sons to fly down on their school vacation. They will then escort Mom back up north with them. I am so relieved to find a solution and eagerly look forward to the time when I will once again be alone. I feel at this time, that I am able to still care for myself. I also think that through my solitude, I will shed my deep-seated anger that has taken over my ability to reason.

I dream I am staying at a retreat center. The interaction with the people who have attended the retreat is so real and mature that I am not sure if I am really dreaming. A strong male teacher tells me I will be making some big life changes and he holds me gently as we sway together in an embrace. I feel the welcome male energy and I begin to cry real tears.

I continually pray to be given that which will help me to see. I question what this blindness is about. The nagging thoughts of past religious training in my childhood come up and I ask, "Why am I being punished? What am I not seeing? What is it that I need to see? Do I need to go deep within to see what it is? Do I need to prove my trust in God?" I feel the need to meditate on all the blindness in the world. I decide I will pray for the physically, the emotionally and the spiritually blind everywhere. If I can help in any way to raise the collective unconscious and bring in the light to others, perhaps that is my purpose here in this life. With this realization comes renewed hope, and I find peace.

I find I can no longer walk unescorted, nor can I ride my bike or drive my car. Painting is impossible because I cannot see the colors on the palette. I reluctantly cancel the painting and drawing lessons I have been giving to the children in the area. My computer becomes my friend and I link up with others through email. I am grateful that I took Miss Dixon's typing class in high school. She covered all the letters and numbers on the keyboards until their location became second nature to my fingers. Now I can type with my eyes closed and then let my spell check correct the spelling errors. It does take time to read the incoming mail but my need to communicate with the outside world outweighs the discomfort. The need to write is pervasive. I am typing short essays of thoughts and ideas running through my mind.

Some of my colleagues who are massage therapists have begun to take turns coming to my house to work on me. It is a team effort, all of us working on my healing. I am grateful for those friends. It is their inspiration that keeps me going. The vision of Humpty Dumpty falling off the wall comes to mind. I am barely hanging on the wall by one clenched hand. I fear the fall because I am not sure that anyone including God or myself will be able to put me back together again. I still hold onto that thin thread of control. I still cannot see the way to detach and completely let myself go.

Luckily, I have written favorite phrases and Bible verses in my journals over the years. Although it is challenging to read them even with the aid of a magnifying glass and abundant patience, they mean a great deal to me. Those affirmations form the thread of my continual conversation with my Creator. Even as I try to bring myself closer to

God, the illusion of separation between us seems to widen due to my inability to let go.

My moods have become cyclic. One day I am filled with anger, driving myself to work on the computer or clean the house, do yard work or strain to read a few pages. Then as I burn out and beat myself up some more, the despondency crawls all over me, dragging its dark blanket of depression with it. Gradually, I am sinking deeper into despair and self-pity.

Oddly enough, real tears flow freely when I weep. I question my doctor about this phenomena and he tells me that there are two separate tear sources; one for routine lubrication and one for the tears associated with emotional release. My eyes actually feel much better when I cry. I find I am able to arouse my emotional response enough to weep freely throughout each day to enable me to walk about the house, dial the phone or read my mail.

The periods of despair seem to be lengthening as the winter wears on. I look forward to my family's arrival for a visit and my mother's departure. The strength of my faith in my Creator is always there with me but I cannot seem to grasp the teachings that have sustained me and allowed me to grow in spirit for the last six years. Therefore, I remain separate and isolated from Creator. I find it takes a superhuman effort to meditate. My prayer consists of the mantra: "I can't do this, God."

The owls call nightly. They seem to be close by my window. The owls symbolize beginnings and endings, changes or death. I know that the person I have been up until now is dying. I don't believe I ever knew that dying to self would be so terribly painful. Yogananda says, "If you live with the Lord, you will be healed of the delusions of life and death, health and sickness. Be in the Lord. Feel His love, fear nothing. Only in the castle of God can we find protection. There is no safer haven of joy than in His presence. When you are with Him, nothing can touch you."

There is one meditation that works for me. It is the personal pyramid image. I envision a beautiful pyramid of my own design on a sandy desert. I walk toward my pyramid slowly with the warm breezes blowing my thin white gauze blouse and skirt about my legs. I carry a large brimmed hat in my hand. As I reach the door of my pyramid, I glance upward to a marquee above the door where there is a message just for me. The inspirational message changes each time I enter my pyramid. Sometimes, it says, "You are loved" or "Come in and rest, dear one.", Worn smooth by the constant blowing of sand and wind against its surface, the door feels soft to my touch. The ancient iron latch is rubbed smooth and is comfortable in my hand as I swing the door open and slip into the quiet cool sanctuary. My shoes and hat are left by the door. Immediately I move to the center of the large room where there is a golden bed, with golden coverlets and fine pillows. Above the bed there is a beam of golden light streaming in from an unseen source. I sit in the middle of the golden light in the bed and bask in the glow of loving warmth. I allow it to envelop and energize me. I realize everything I need in this life is right here now. All I need to do is sit in this Light. Eventually, I quietly slip out of the golden bed, pick up my shoes and hat and move outside. This meditation has proved so useful to me that I continue to use it.

As a Seeker, I journey thus far.
Having come to this place,
I set out once again.

MARCH

Lord, how daunting the armies massed against me!
All of them jeer at me,
"God will not save you."

PSALMS 3:2-3

The loons have arrived here in Broad Creek. I hear them calling nearby in the hours before dawn. Huge flocks of ducks migrating north stopped here in our Creek for a few days to rest and renew their energy before the remainder of their flight to northern nesting grounds. A great horned owl calls in the twilight from a tree across the Creek. I can hear the answer from its mate a distance away. I have always kept a diary of natural happenings throughout the seasons no matter where I am living. I scribble down what I can barely see but can hear and identify. I am frustrated because I can no longer see through my spotting scope or through the binoculars.

My neighbor has volunteered to drive the twenty-seven miles to the airport to pick up my daughter and her children. Suddenly my house is an explosion of youthful energy. It is a fine symphony to my ears. I am able to cook most of the meals for my family with my daughter's help. My car is not large enough to accommodate six people so Mom and I take turns going out with the family to the beach, museums and the aquarium. My daughter appears to be very stressed from her recent separation. She had been living with my husband at our Vermont home on the Lake but since it was sold, she has moved into a smaller rental cottage in the area. I am filled with sadness at the changes taking place in our family.

I have always read to the boys and it pains me to tell them I cannot do so. But they tease and beg until I finally begin to make up stories. Initially, my heart is not really into it but their enthusiasm overcomes my discomfort as I weave a tale. They go from story telling to adventures outside on the Creek. I have an aluminum rowboat that takes on the majesty and excitement of a large ship when propelled by two young boys. My kayak is delivered but I don't have a safe way to launch it down over the riprap-lined shore. The boys are inventive and suggest I cover a long board with carpet so that the kayak will slide down it ramp fashion and not be scratched by the rocks on our shoreline. They have a great curiosity about crabbing. So we set the crab trap out in the Creek baiting it with fried chicken, of all things. Each day the two oldest boys row out to check the trap's contents. Nothing is lured into that trap by fried chicken. Apparently, crabs don't appreciate southern fried chicken as human beings do. Actually, I am told that the crabs are buried deep in the layers of mud this time of year.

Launch day arrives for the kayak and me. With ample assistance and cameras at ready, I gingerly climb in. I am pushed off and find myself gloriously free and floating gently in the brown water that is our Creek. I paddled out away but as then the wind picked up. It took several attempts to bring the tender kayak in to the shore without tipping over. My family members stood ready to steady the boat while I stepped out, then they hauled it up the ramp. This appears to be quite challenging and something I will not be able to do alone. Frustration knocked the wind out of my sails as I put the boat back in the basement.

My family left a couple of days ago. I am up and out in the predawn hours, the breathtaking colors of the Glory Glow mirrored on the creek. I carry the boat to the water; slide it gently down until just the bow is held on the edge of the ramp. At my first attempt to climb in, the blasted kayak flips upside down so quickly I don't have much time to realize what has happened to me until I feel the icy water on my back. Stubbornly, I have decided I can lick this tender little banana boat but not until I have changed my clothing. I give it another go. This time,

I am successful in the launching process but in the back of my mind, I wonder how I will bring it back in. I paddle out along the shoreline of Broad Creek singing at the top of my lungs. Singing actually seems to help keep my eyes open. When I can no longer think of songs I know, I make them up. I find that I am singing my story to all that will listen. It feels exquisite to connect with the water, this deep, dark feminine creative energy source. I made the decision to name the boat, Namaskar, a Sanskrit word meaning, "I celebrate and honor the Divine in all things." I am being rocked and buoyed by my beloved gentle Earth Mother. My mind takes me back to a canoe trip taken with two friends in Maine a year or so ago.

On an energizing clear moonlight night in Cape Elizabeth, two friends, Claude and Phil, shared with me a canoe trip out through the marshes on a tidal creek. There was darkness after the bright clear, warming sunshine earlier on the beach. The sun disappeared leaving behind an expressionistic painting of color and shade—mysterious purple, pink all dusty and gray on the edges but brilliant elsewhere with the promise of light behind the low clouds, the fear and anticipation of the coming period of darkness. The wonderment: What will it be like? How will it feel? How long will it last? Will I be cold? Not wanting to let go of the light and color but knowing it was inevitable. Knowing we must do so to move on in time. The glow gradually receded and grew dim.

In a metaphoric sense, I stood prepared to enter the vehicle that would carry me on the stream eventually to the Light, to Earth Mother, to Moon Wisdom, riding the black, saline fluid of our Earth Mother's womb.

As I waited in the darkness, I watched for any indication of the light, the promise. Anxiety crept in along with the increasing darkness and the cold. I began to question the importance and necessity of this journey, this life. I settled into thinking of my comfort, of a warm, light-filled shelter and a cup of soothing hot tea. At that moment, behind the low trees of the barrier islands in the east, I saw the first faint glow. As the female corn moon began her rise to our hungry eyes, she first appeared fiery, hot and golden as though she were masquerading as a male.

We climbed into our canoe and were once again cast into darkness. We were below the level of sight. My guides, Claude, and Phil, propelled me smoothly along. We moved quietly and steadily for a time, each of us in our own space alone with our thoughts. The banks of the tidal creek were mysterious to me. They contained many life forms that I could only imagine. I heard various noises and gurgles but was unafraid as I allowed myself to journey on the dark stream of life in trust and faith. I wanted to experience it all. We hesitated a bit as two fellow travelers in another canoe, hit a snag on their journey. We offered guidance and support until they are able to move off on their own, disappearing into the darkness.

As we rounded a bend, we were bathed in the light from our Sister Moon. She showed us a smile from her cratered face. There was still a warm goldeness that remained with her as she moved further away from the exposure to her male counterpart, the Sun.

Soon we slipped into the darkness once again. I still felt no fear. I basked in the memory of the moonlight glow. I trusted that I would soon see and feel it again on this journey. We continued to glide along, winding through the dank and damp world of the birth-like passageway. The resistance increased as we moved closer to the source of the light. The vibration of the incoming tide gurgled beneath our hull. My guides were forced to work harder and be more vigilant to keep me on course as the current increased. They struggled to keep me from hitting the snags, the sand bar or the dark mysterious banks with their hollows and holes.

Once more, my guides brought me into the brilliance of the light. There was a shaft, a moonbeam given to us to light the way for a long distance. We journeyed along in peaceful reverence until time to turn back home.

The returning trip was resistance free as we moved with the tidal current. My guides rested a bit except when the time came to turn a Corner. Sister Moon was well overhead now in her solitary whiteness and her pure light. She was everywhere around me, first on my left, then my right, then over my shoulder and on my back but she was no longer ever in front of me on the journey home.

The scrape of the canoe on the sandy shore brought me quickly back to reality. I climbed out and stood again on firm ground, still breathing in the blessings of it all and gave thanks.

Not long after my accidental dunking in the cold water of Broad Creek, my neighbor John volunteered to build a ladder off my dock for easier access to the tipsy kayak. I have found such caring and concern in this small community. I have received much and have finally let go of keeping track so that I can return the favor. There is no way I can ever repay them for all they have given me during this time of trial. The only way I can ever repay what I have received is to give to others in any way I am able. My prayer list continues to grow and grow.

My eyes are closed much of the time while I am in the kayak but there aren't many obstacles of concern in our creek so I continue to paddle as much as the weather will allow. I find I must go out before the sun rises too high in the sky because the light reflected off the water is unbearable. My little dog, Duffy and the old cat, Pumpkin, sit on the dock while I am gone and await my return. I am always assured a warm welcome home as Duffy nuzzles my hands as I grip the ladder to climb up on the dock.

I feel my physical strength is returning as my fitness level increases. I have always been active and participated in vigorous activities out of doors. I need to move my body and stretch my muscles to feel fully alive. The familiar feeling of soreness in my shoulders and hands makes me feel alive and healthy once more. I am pushing myself relentlessly to get out on the water as much as possible. A few years ago, after selling my dressage horse and leaving my equestrian life behind, I purchased a Nordic Trak exercise machine. After a few months, I became bored with it and decided to sell it. As fate would have it, no one called and it did not sell. Now I find I am able to use it on the days when I cannot go out on the water. Sometimes during my workout, I suddenly find my eyes welling up with tears of grief and I burst into deep gut-wrenching wailing. It is obvious to me that this form of physical exercise is helping me to expel my deep inner sadness and move on. I am feeling much more positive about my life and the possibility of restoring my marriage as March comes to a close.

I am crouched, poised from my fall, ready to leap upward to greater manifestations of my beliefs, my abilities and my self. To leap, much as an athlete must leap to make a basket, or as a horse gathers himself to clear a jump. All of my senses, all my being, and all my muscles, everything in my body are poised ready to make the leap.

"This restriction has shown up in my life to teach me something. When I get the lesson, I will then see my inner faith manifesting itself in positive ways again. I will bless this occurrence rather than curse it, knowing always that the ways of God will sometimes be mysterious to me." Wayne Dyer, *Your Sacred Self*

APRIL

Word I was in the house alone
Somehow must have gotten abroad,
Word I was in my life alone,
Word I had no one left but God.
EXCERPT FROM *"BEREFT"* BY ROBERT FROST

At last I am alone. I am grateful for Duffy and Pumpkin. Without them, I would not climb out of bed, but they demand to be let out, to be let in and to be fed. Getting out of bed and walking the length of the house arouses my physical needs, such as hunger and thirst. Preparing food has become a new challenge. I prepare very simple meals, often just cereal and fruit. When my husband was here he helped me build a raised garden in the back of the house. It was one of the last things he did for me. I have planted as many vegetables as I can possibly cram into the space. I look forward to eating from my mini-garden in another few weeks. My shelves are stocked with canned goods but I cannot see to prepare anything that requires measuring, pouring or cooking. One night as I set about to prepare some sautéed chicken breast to put on a green salad, I set the quart bottle of olive oil on the counter after pouring a small amount into the pan. I didn't see that I had set the glass bottle too close to the edge. Actually, I think it may have been teetering on the edge when I hit it lightly with my hand. It shattered into a million pieces coated and mingled with the oil on the ceramic tile floor. I sat on the floor and sobbed in frustration and anger. I had to clean it up immediately because I couldn't reach the stove to shut off the chicken. What a challenge to clean up the greasy substance and pick up all the shards without cutting my hands and knees. It took me roughly an hour and a half to clean up the mess. I slipped and slid around on that floor for a week afterward until I found a cleaning person to come in and help me out.

Cooking has always been a passion of mine. Now it is one more creative outlet that is not available to me. I enjoy eating well and find pleasure in feeding others. Even when the children were young, I attempted to expose them to the different tastes of various countries. They enjoyed it and so did I as it gave me another vent for my creativity. Only through my creative expression was I able to ease the drudgery of childcare and housekeeping. During the early years of being a parent I began to express myself on canvas. I left the dishes in the sink until morning so I could stay up later to lose myself in my artwork while the children slept. I found myself very anxious to put them to bed each night so I could escape the mundane and the ordinary to drift off in the meditative singularity of the creative process.

My home in North Carolina has many windows to enable the viewer to witness all that happens out on the creek and in the fields and marshes surrounding the house. I never thought I would want to shut out the glorious light that streams into the house from early morning until sundown but now my eyes have become so light-sensitive that I am forced to buy shades for all the windows. I tried many different types of sunglasses including goggles but nothing really offers the protection from light and air that would enable me to see in comfort. It becomes a joke with my friends that I have become a lady of the night. Actually, I find that the darkness does not offer comfort either.

My neighbors continue to call inquiring if there is anything they can pick up for me when they go to town. I find that it is easier now for me to ask for their help because I feel their caring and concern. I no longer feel compelled to keep track of favors so I can return them to even the score as I always have in the past. I have learned to receive and in doing so, my heart has soothed.

I remember a Polarity session I had midway through my first year of energy work. As I drifted off into a deep relaxed state while the therapist held my head, I began a shamanic journey to the four chambers of the heart. The first chamber was the Chamber of Darkness. I am an infant. I discover I have a severe wound in my heart. A wise medicine woman came with me on this journey. She is the vision of myself as a medicine woman from another time. Her hair is long and white. She wears it in one single braid down her back. Her costume is a white doeskin tunic and leggings. She wears a brilliant crystal necklace with shells and bones on either side. I am struck by her beauty and the light radiating from the brown leathery face. She is surrounded by a luminous energetic force of dancing colors and light. I realize I am being cradled in her strong arms while my heart lies open and bleeding. We travel together to the second chamber, the Chamber of Fire. I see a large blazing fire. Out of the fire rises the figure of darkness. He is suddenly transmuted into a huge grizzly bear. I witness these things but I feel no fear, only comfort and abundant love. He is in the fire and I recall that it is he who has wounded me. As I gaze on his form, I see that he too, has a large gaping wound in his heart. He seems to be very angry. In this chamber I notice other children roaming around. There is a faceless man off to my right but he carries a deep heart wound as well. I notice a teenager with a severely wounded heart. Medicine woman is holding me while tending to all of us. We move to the next chamber, the Chamber of Light. She begins to heal all of us as well as the great bear. She chants and strokes us lightly. She gently places healing poultices made of herbs and quartz crystals over our wounds. The energy of the poultices and the crystal fragments dance in the light that surrounds us. I witness colors beautiful and new to my eyes. I lose track of the faceless man in this chamber. The great bear holds me close. I breathe his breath deep within me. My heart expands and opens with love for the bear. I have so much more light and breath in my heart than I ever felt before. I hear a sweet song that I have heard before long ago. It is then that I realize that medicine woman is my original healing mother. I have been searching for her for lifetimes and at last I have found her. She is the beginning of my long line of medicine women healers. I am so moved, the poultices feel so wonderful, I sob with joy. As she strokes me she removes a sword from my right shoulder that had been there through many lives causing me chronic pain. We move on to the fourth chamber, the Chamber of Gifts. She gently holds my shoulders. I can feel my angel wings expanding. They have been severely clipped. I begin to feel them opening out to a wide span, graceful and strong. I am given the understanding of the purpose of my wide strong shoulders to carry these wings. I also feel little wings on my Achilles tendons that enable me to fly. I see all my treasures, my beauty, and my talents. All that I have been given is revealed to me. I am so grateful, so fulfilled and energized in this chamber of gifts. Medicine woman gently touches my cheek, then places her hand on my heart center, looks deeply into my eyes and bids me farewell.

It took several days for me to process and journal that session. It has changed my life. I felt deeply grounded and connected to earth's energy. My shoulder no longer hurt and I had a much greater range of motion. The deep sadness and resulting pain I had felt so often in my heart and solar plexus was gone. My love for all there is, was expanded. I seemed to have received a deep knowing that I could not explain to anyone. It was just there.

Within a few days after Joe left for Vermont, he mailed me a separation agreement. A few pages of print stating the rules we agree to abide by while we remain separate and apart. I am appalled to realize that a form taken from a legal book of common forms can disconnect my long relationship with this person. The sentence that stands out in my mind says that we will live as single people, allowing us to date others. I have remained in a kind of numb state until late tonight. I have been sitting in my bed next to a lighted candle praying when I realize this is not what I want after all. I feel I have suddenly found the gift of sight through the darkness. I needed to look deep in my heart. It wasn't until I received the separation papers that I realized the truth. I cannot go through with this; I do not want a divorce. We haven't tried counseling recently mainly because of my resistance. I am so deeply involved in my own healing, learning and my work that I felt we would be better off with individual therapy. I feel I have strayed too far afield in my world. I need to come back to my divinity, to the Christ Consciousness, to my daily reading of the scriptures and other spiritual writings. I am infused with the realization that I desperately want to work on my marriage. I begin to make plans to pack up immediately and leave for Vermont to join my husband in a united effort to renew our love for each other. We could begin therapy together as soon as I return. I vow I will do whatever it takes to accomplish what I now believe to be true. Even though it is late, I cannot wait to tell Joe of this epiphany so I excitedly pick up the telephone and dial our home in Vermont. It is always a shock when my own voice comes on the answering machine. I leave a stuttering brief message and hang up. Surely there is an explanation for his not being at home. I will try again before dawn since my mind is racing wildly and I can't sleep. I am confronted with the obvious when my calls continue to go unanswered. I fall into a deep depression. I drag myself from bed to turn on the word processor and write my husband a letter. I send it off through the email at dawn. He telephones a couple of days later to say that he has thought long and hard on what I have proposed but feels that "he needs to get on with his life" and therefore does not want any reconciliation.

Humpty Dumpty fell down off the wall she was clinging to. She fell hard and shattered into a million fragments of herself much like the olive oil jar had shattered a few days before. Reality has chosen to deal with me harshly. I wait a few days before I call him to beg him to reconsider. I don't ever recall begging for anything in my life. I mistakenly thought only his approval and his efforts could put me back together again. After my second pleading call, his answer came swift and certain. No, he was going on his way.

My spirit has faded; I am in a place of darkness and despair. I realize that I have been abandoned, that I am sick and nearly blind, and I feel old and useless. All sense of self seems to have left me. I feel alone, separate from everyone, even God. There does not seem to be any path open to me. I cannot serve God in the state I am in. I am useless, unloved and unwanted by my husband and by my family. I have made the decision to end my life. I will take a vacuum cleaner hose and duck tape it to the exhaust pipe on my car, stick it in the window, taping carefully around the window so there aren't any leaks. I do not want to fail. No one will find me for days because I have very little company. Therefore, I feel the need to take the dog and cat with me. They have been with me through so much up to this point; it seems only fitting to journey to the other side together. As I lie in my bed planning, two obstacles come to mind: First, the vacuum hose will have to be borrowed from the nearby Baptist Church because I don't have one. I have borrowed that machine before to blow up my air mattress for the grandchildren to sleep on when they visit. That means, I will have to drive the half-mile to the church, get the hose and return to do the installation. I am not sure I can drive to the end of the driveway at this point. The second obstacle is I cannot just leave without an explanation to all those who love me. How will my family and friends react to my sudden, unexplained exit? I must write some notes. I begin the task of explaining to each one. As I write each of my loved ones, it is becoming an act of offering up my burdens to my Creator. Fatigue has overcome me and I am transported to that blessed dream state.

I dreamed my husband had given me a brand new blue car. For some reason, I left it in a deserted gravel pit. I locked it and walked home. The next day, deep snow covered everything. I walked down to get the car and it was gone. There was a clear set of ATV tracks coming in to the pit area. Curiously, there were no car tracks. I had left nothing of mine in the car. I walked back home and called my husband. He accepted the news of the car's disappearance with a grunt.

This morning during the Glory Glow following my attempt at suicide, the ringing of the phone rouses me from sleep. It is my friend Nicky from Massachusetts calling to see how I am. At the sound of her voice, the Light of blessedness surrounds me and I look up from my dark despair towards my Creator. I give thanks once again to be alive.

In I Peter I read, "You may have had to suffer grief in all kinds of trials. These have come so that your faith may be proved genuine and may result in praise, glory and honor when Jesus Christ is revealed." Also in I Peter," . . . being tested as fire tests gold and purifies it—and your faith is far more precious to God than mere gold; so if your faith remains strong after being tried in the test tube of fiery trials, it will bring you much praise and glory and honor on the day of the return."

The questions that haunt me now are: Who will love me? Who will want me? What can I do? Where will I go? All these questions coming from a needy being who has always relied on someone else to define who she is and what it is that instills her with happiness.

I realize I will have to hire an attorney to represent my interest in this failed marriage. I ask friends but none of my current friends and neighbors have ever been faced with a divorce. I have turned to the yellow pages. Names, so many names, but none of them seem to stand out. In frustration, I slam the phone book down and leave that decision for another day.

One of my daughters and her husband and children are due for a visit. They have offered to drive me to Duke Medical Center in Raleigh for the appointment I have with a rheumatologist regarding the diagnosis of Sjogrens Syndrome. I am looking forward to seeing my two grandchildren. Their love and affection for me is beautiful and honest. They arrive and settle in. After the children are in bed, I sit with my daughter and her husband and tell them of our pending divorce. My daughter shocks and saddens me with the intensity of her response. Her angry remarks are directed at me but I can see that she is responding from a place of fear. She is hard at work in her life and doesn't want the responsibility of caring for a single disabled parent. But I am left with feelings of being unlovable, undeserving and more desolate than I had ever felt before. The drive to Duke is strained and long for all of us. My ability to use my eyes is minimal. My son-in-law and my grandchildren guide me.

Their visit was short and after they left, I felt a sense of relief. I began the task of telling my other three children the news of separation over the telephone. My son remarked that he was not surprised. He said he had been expecting it because my husband and I had spent so much time apart. Although their reactions are not angry or accusatory, I feel very little compassion or support. They appear to not feel my sorrow, fear or pain. I find myself falling down into the fiery furnace of transformation once again. I begin preparing my death. And just as before, when I reach those dark walls where there appears to be no way out, a telephone call from another dear friend points the way back to the Light. God is always here ready to pull me back up on my feet when I am ready.

Early one morning as I am meditating, the name of a Polarity therapist whom I met at a seminar a year earlier flashed upon the inner screen of my mind. Whenever this happens to me, I have learned to follow up on my intuition immediately. As I rummage through the old business cards I have saved, doubt begins creeping in. When I find her card, I hold it in my hand for a long while. I realize how limited my options appear to be at this time. With magnifying glass in hand, I hesitantly dial the phone. The most amazing thing happens; Vera answers the phone in person rather than an answering machine picking up the call. I probably would not have left a message or even called her back a second time if I'd thought about what I was doing. I only met her briefly and spent a few hours working with her but something about her had stuck with me. She is working at a place called the Sanctuary, which is a place of integrative healing. I explain briefly what is happening in my life and ask her if she knows of anyone who could help me through this spiritual and physical emergency. Then the second amazing thing occurs, she said, "I will come right down and pick you up. You can stay here with me for a week or more and receive healing sessions from several different therapists." Before I had time to think about it, I accept her invitation, make hurried arrangements for my pets. Then before I can change my mind, I find myself practically poured into her vehicle for the three-hour drive to Raleigh, North Carolina.

My eyes remain closed for the entire trip. I don't feel any fear or apprehension about spending a week with a near stranger in a strange place. Gratefully, I realize I just made my first leap of faith, many more will follow. Vera sleeps on the office floor so that I can have her bed and room. Even in my fragile state of numbness, I begin to feel safe and loved. I leave Sanctuary only once during my weeklong stay here—to have lunch out with my rescuing angel. It is a celebration of my return to life. During the day when I am not having a massage or Polarity session, I am curled up in a large recliner near the huge window overlooking the ivy-covered garden. I sleep most of the time in this chair but I do try to listen to inspirational audio tapes. My week at Sanctuary is uplifting and allows me time to strengthen my inner self. But it is necessary for me to return home and face my relationship concerns. Vera later tells me how shocked she was when she arrived at my home to pick me up that morning. She had remembered from our meeting two years ago, someone entirely different than the thin, drawn, pathetic person who seemed ravaged from rapid aging in just one year.

I have decided to try to connect with my mentor, the Japanese woman who came to meet me in Boston a few years earlier. I rarely can reach her with the first call because she travels all over the world teaching. But she says she was just on her way out the door when she heard the phone ring so she picked it up. As always, she instills in me that "I am the radiant love of the Source". That I continue "to blossom as a unique and beautiful flower in the cosmic garden". She also tells me that "compassion is born of sorrow, mercy is compassion in action". I listen and I weep.

It is the end of the month and I have received a letter from the rheumatologist at Duke. According to the blood tests, they are unable to determine if I do have Sjogrens. It seems that testing for Sjogrens is not accurate for sometime often years. Most doctors rely on the symptoms. It states, that I have severe dry eye and am to be referred to a cornea specialist also at Duke. He also says he feels many of the symptoms I have will abate once I am able to go beyond the present state of my personal life. I am certainly manifesting the physical symptoms of my shattered blind trust and faith that I have applied to my relationship with my husband. I am a somatic healer and regularly feel the pain and blockages in energy flow of others in my own body in varying degrees of intensity. I haven't realized before that I have been bringing my own blockages, dreams and visions into physical manifestation through the illness in my body. I am experiencing dreams where I am witnessing some act, then realize upon waking that I am actually bleeding or bruised from projecting the action onto my physical form. These dreams are happening in the energetic field, and then as they are reduced in vibration, they actually show up as physical symptoms.

My friend from Maine is here to visit. While she is here, we drive to Duke for my meeting with the recommended cornea specialist. We climb out of bed at 4:30 a.m. to arrive on time for the appointment. The doctor is surly, abrupt and disinterested. He basically tells me I have dry eyes and need to learn to live with it. I am furious as I walk out of there but I am not ready to give up hope that there is help for me out there somewhere.

The doctor I saw while at the Sanctuary had suggested that I might be suffering from heavy metal poisoning. That makes sense to me because I suffered from fish poisoning in the Virgin Islands in the early eighties. Some of the fish feed off the mercury and lead leaching off the bottoms of the rotting hulls of sunken war ships. Most of the fishermen don't fish near the wrecks but occasionally a contaminated fish will be caught. After experiencing the initial acute flu-like symptoms of fever, digestive pain, vomiting, diarrhea, joint aches, I found that the joint discomfort, swelling of the joints, irregular gait, and numbness stayed with me for about two years. I became severely limited in my ability to walk any distance or stay on my feet without severe pain. I was forced to give up horseback riding and jogging. The out-of-doors sports that I had always excelled in were too painful to do. I suffered with arthritis-like pain and stiffness in my hips, shoulders and fingers. Notably, these are the very same symptoms of Sjogrens as well. I was 42 years old but felt much as I do now, that my life as I knew it was over.

It was actually the pain in my hips that brought me to North Carolina in 1989. It became increasingly difficult for me to move freely about during the cold damp weather of a Vermont winter. Joe and I had talked about it and because I was devoting all of my time to my artwork and teaching art privately, we felt I could come south for the cold months to paint. The first year, I stayed only a month but it was such a pleasurable and productive period that the next year, we rented a condo for three months. My husband would come visit every other week or so and stay for a few days. He expressed how much joy it brought him to have a break from the winter weather up north every couple of weeks. It shortened and brightened the winter for him too. He appeared to really enjoy eastern North Carolina as much as I did. We bought land and a boat slip while dreaming of retiring in Oriental where we could sail our boat all year long. After five years of renting for the winter, we purchased another piece of land in Whortonsville, a quaint fishing and farming village just off the Neuse River and Pamlico Sound. We began the process of planning and building our retirement home.

I spent the entire winter with a designer who worked with our plans and ideas. I had been gathering photos, drawings and plans from architectural magazines. I knew what I wanted in a house but I needed to put it all together. We envisioned working from our home so we each needed work space apart from one another. He decided he would sign up for some psychology classes. Combined with his many years as a lawyer and a judge, we could work together as team healers. He in the counseling side of it and me doing the hands-on energetic body work. It sure sounded great to me at that point although we had never actually spent a great deal of time working closely with each other. I had worked on and off in his office filing or answering the phone but never on a full-time basis. As I write this, I have rethought of our dream of working together. I realize that the few times we tried teamwork such as on our sailboat, we failed miserably.

Our land is shaped like an arrow facing the water. The house plans were drawn to follow the contour of the land, thus allowing for a view of the water from nearly every window. It didn't seem to be an accident that the arrow shape appeared to form a bridge between what would become a healing center and the church across the fields representing the community. I visualized a rainbow bridge of light between the community and the work that I was called to do here.

The center of the house is the community room while the wings became workspace for each of us, plus bedrooms. It is built high in the air on pilings with a hip roof that will deflect the high winds we often get. This was the first time I had ever built a house from scratch and was not prepared for the detailed decisions that had to be made as the construction progressed. It was exhausting. My partner was allowed me to take charge of the project without interference. He took charge of the financial end of it. Like magic, it grew and came into being. It represented an art form for me. As I perched on a cinder block in the briar-infested empty lot, I had promised God that this house, if it were to become a reality, would be devoted to healing and spirituality. Each month as I made my way south to inspect the progress, I approached it with a mixture of reverence and awe as I witnessed a sculptural miracle that was taking form between the marshes and the Creek's edge.

After they had set the pilings, it was as though an ancient pagan worship site had been reproduced; perhaps a place to worship the goddess of water, Thetis, mother of Achilles. On one of my trips, the framework was constructed up to the sub-flooring. The workmen put down a ladder and offered me a hand enabling me to stand in what would be my living room. Tears of joy flowed as I stood there in the sunshine twelve feet up off the earth without any walls or other obstructions to interrupt the view. Everywhere I could see there was water, marsh, pines and the white spire of the little church across the field. What a shame we must build walls that block our being able to see what inspires us and brings us such joy. In the design of the house, I tried to keep walls to a minimum for that very reason. In our lives, we must keep walls to a minimum as well. We certainly need clear boundaries but the solid walls that serve only to cut us off from our inspiration, from our God, our life force, are not needed for support after we have been lifted to a place of clear vision.

The house progressed according to schedule and we moved in shortly after the first of the New Year. Our furniture was delayed in a blizzard in New England but that time spent in spaciousness within the house allowed me to adjust to the newness of this place that was to be my home, my sanctuary and eventually, my monastery. My husband could not stay for the arrival of the furniture therefore it was up to me to move in and settle our things into their new places. I found living high off the ground had its disadvantages when there are many boxes and objects that need to be brought upstairs. I settled the house as quickly as I could but was totally exhausted by my efforts. I believed the quicker I got settled, the more time I would have to enjoy my new home and surroundings before it was springtime and therefore, time to return to Vermont.

The previous September, I along with two crew members, had brought our sailboat, *Nepenthe,* south along the intercoastal waterway route. My crew was composed of friends from our yacht club in Vermont. Joe joined us for part of the trip. It was roughly one thousand miles and took about a month to complete. We basically took our time, staying in some favorite spots on the Chesapeake Bay for a few days at a time. Coming out of Lake Champlain, the mast and all the rigging required to hold it up had to be stepped down on the deck because of the low clearance under a few bridges in the Champlain Canal. The mast was put back up in Catskill, New York on the Hudson River. Twelve locks had to be negotiated to reach clear water in the Hudson River at Troy,

New York. Even though I had made the trip before, it was still an exciting adventure. However, by the time we reached my home dock in North Carolina, I was very tired and worn. I decided there was no way I would ever do it again without Joe's help. The responsibility and work involved was just too much for me at that time.

We had scheduled a charter on a sailboat with friends in Martinique, French West Indies, in March for three weeks. The time I had to spend in North Carolina enjoying my new home was shortened. The first week in February, I had taken my little dog, Duffy, to the beach where he thoroughly explored the sea grass and the dunes. A few days later I noticed a red lump on his gum line. A trip to the vet revealed that it was not the suspected sandspur but a cancerous growth. The vet recommended immediate surgery to biopsy and remove the tumor. After the surgery, she sadly reported that she had been unable to remove all the mass and made several suggestions involving rather invasive treatments, none of which guaranteed anything. I was deeply saddened but felt that Duffy would be happier living his life for whatever length it was to be without the sickness and debilitation that comes with cancer treatment. I was advised that he probably had another three to six months to live. He was only five years old at that time. Since I could not reconcile leaving him with a pet sitter for three weeks while I sailed merrily around the Caribbean, I told my husband I would not go. He was very upset by my decision and in the end, persuaded me to go. It was with great sadness that I left my little friend that day to fly off to meet my husband and friends in Puerto Rico. He was left with a close friend who had permission to euthanize him if necessary as well as instructions on the disposition of his remains if it should come to that. I promised to call every other day to check the state of his health. The other two couples we were chartering with were close sailing buddies of Duffy who had known him since his puppy days on board our boat. Duffy has made many human friends.

Shortly after arriving in Marin, Martinque, we did some sightseeing on a bus. One trip took us to a cathedral high on a mountainside. The cathedral was a diminutive duplicate of the famous Chartres cathedral in France. The six of us treaded reverently up to the altar where we each lit a candle and prayed on our knees for the life of "Mr. Duffy". I attempted to call many times from the French islands but found it was next to impossible to call out. I was quite frustrated and concerned but finally reached home to find that he was fine and dandy. His condition remained consistent throughout my absence. That entire episode occurred six years ago at this writing. Mr. Duffy is still well and as spirited as any Welsh terrier can be even at age eleven. The power of prayer is magical.

Six years have also passed since the house was built. Some things have changed but others have not. Dennis Augustine wrote in *Invisible Means of Support*, "The oneness in everything is true reality; everything else is Maya (illusion). A dream of which we are capable of awakening." I ask myself when will I awaken from this bad dream.

> *For death remembered should be like a mirror*
> *Who tells us life's but breath, to trust it error.*
> WILLIAM SHAKESPEARE

MAY

When we were children, on May 1, my grandmother would walk with us out into the woods and swamps near the farmhouse and there would instruct us to pick bouquets of wild flowers, filling the baskets we had saved from Easter. She would then drive us around town where there were people who were not able to leave their homes because of age or illness. We would scamper across the yard, up on the porch as quietly as we could. As we placed the wild flower baskets beside the door, we rang the bell or knocked on the door and then ran as fast as we could for Grandma's discreetly parked car. What a beautiful gift of sharing Grandma had given us!

The coming of May this year has not brought visions of wild flowers but a vision of a ship filled with my children and grandchildren being tossed about on a stormy sea until at last it heaves a great sigh and breaks up in pieces sinking to the bottom. I have clung to the huge wheel trying to hold the ship on course but the storm is too great. We are totally out of control. There is no steerage, no rudder. My loved ones are separated and blown away from one another. I cannot find them, I hear their cries but I cannot see them. We are tossed and battered by the wind and the sea. I pray and beg for mercy as I sadly watch the large ship's wheel, of which I am the hub, break apart. Eventually, the seas calm and the sun comes out. I am alone for a time until I feel a familiar hand grasp mine. At last I have found part of my family and we are reunited. Gradually, more and more family members find one another. Over time we will all be reunited once more. We swim to shore and plant our feet firmly on the earth. We speak of our story, our wounds and our survival. We will be different from what we were before the devastation of the storm but I know we will be stronger. Our scars will exist only to remind us of the preciousness of each shared moment in our lives. A new vision of the wheel appears now with God at the hub, as it should be. I am out in the wheel now sharing my strength with my loved ones. This is the place where I need to be now. We will float once more in our restored and strengthened family ship upon the creative waters of life.

This morning during prayer, I ask for support in a very material sense. I ask to be given nutritious taste-tempting food. Due to my inability to see, my meals are very simple and boring. I generally pick greens from the garden, and then sauté either cut-up chicken or tofu to create a salad. I have an automatic rice steamer so I eat rice almost every day. Day after day of the same diet is adding to my depressed state of mind but there seems little I can do to change it.

I am stirred from my meditations this afternoon, by the ringing of the doorbell. A young woman in an apron stands in the open doorway, holding a large tray of food. I weep openly at the sight of this angel bearing food. I thank her while mumbling something about her being a messenger from God but my tears and the smells wafting from the Styrofoam containers force me to close the door and make for the kitchen as fast as a nearly blind woman can. A special person who is a chef at a local restaurant has sent the food. God has spoken to her and she has supplied me with enough food for several meals. Actually, more food comes every few days until I leave to go to the north for the summer.

The same day I had prayed for food, I had also prayed for a teacher. Just as the food appeared, so did my teacher, Mary, who has since become a beloved friend. I received a telephone call with a soft female voice greeting me. She tells me many people have said she needs to meet me. She has made the effort. She wonders if we could meet for tea. I ask her to come out to my home this afternoon. During our conversation, I discover she is a healer of souls, a deeply spiritual person, and a former nun, a person of magic, a therapist and a teacher. Again, my prayer is answered as our friendship grows. Her guidance and love uplifts me and spurs me onward as the painful process of dying to my self and to my old thought forms continues. Sometimes we just sit quietly as she reads to me. I am thirsty for mental stimulation at this point; she has brought water to a parched spirit. Knowing she is available to me on the other end of the phone line is a precious safety line that I can grasp if I need it. She works with me on interpreting the numerous dreams recorded in my journal. Through the dream work, I am able to see that I am working through a process and am exactly where God wants me to be, doing exactly what I need to do at this particular time.

During meditation, the image of myself as a two-fisted eraser comes to me. There I am busily wiping away any leftover residue with an eraser in each hand. I have always used affirmations and found them to be quite effective in changing old thought patterns that we often become stuck with. I use the following affirmations frequently through this period of my journey:

I am not a hostage.
I am not a co-dependant.
I am true to myself.
I have found my voice.
I will survive.
All things may be destroyed including my body but I will survive.
All my choices fully support and enhance
my life force and my divine nature.

From the book, *God Calling,* channeled from a Higher Being through two English women and edited by A.J.Russell, the following lines helped to sustain me and gave me courage to go on: "I shall guide you one day at a time. And for each day, I shall supply the wisdom and the strength. Never let one day pass when you have not reached out an arm of love to someone outside your home. Be full of joy, love and laugh, I am with you. To dwell in thought on the material, when once you lived with me is to call it into being. So you must be careful only to think of and desire that which will help, not hinder your spiritual growth. The same law operates too on the spiritual plane. Think love and love surrounds you, and all about whom you think. Think thoughts of ill will and ill surrounds you and those about whom you think. Think health and health comes. The physical reflects the mental and the spiritual."

I am no stranger to pain, having birthed four children naturally, survived many injuries from my equestrian days, and suffered severe migraines combined with joint/muscle pain for much of my life. Yet, this deep heart pain is almost unbearable, the price of an inexhaustible open heart. I can relate this open-heart vulnerability to my dressage riding a few years ago. I had ridden various seats throughout my life-long riding experience from bareback, saddle seat to forward seat. They all require balance but also some gripping with the thighs and knees. When riding dressage seat, it is important to be relaxed and perfectly balanced. The aids the rider gives the horse are very subtle. The rider's legs are allowed to be long and quite relaxed. Dressage is a beautiful and graceful way of communicating with the horse on a higher plane. It is like dancing with the horse. As a consequence, if the horse should shy suddenly, the rider is very often left in the dirt. If the rider becomes fearful and tightens up all the grace and beauty disappear. I see the similarity between this lesson in riding and the tight gripping, fearful heart as compared with the fluid grace and open communication of the more beautiful but vulnerable open heart. It seems far better to chance the deep heart pain occasionally than to be blocked and closed. I practice breathing through my heart chakra, allowing the light and the breath to enter through my crown chakra, flow down past my brow chakra or third eye, past my throat chakra to my heart chakra; breathing in on the left side of the vortex and out on the right, continuing this exercise until I feel the spreading warmth and expansion in my entire chest cavity. This is medicine and will lessen the pain but one must allow the cause of the pain to be transmuted to Light and Love. We are all fine instruments of our Creator's power and we must trust that

God will not allow us to be damaged by remaining too long in the fire of transmutation. It seems that I am thrust into the fire periodically, then pulled, allowed to cool, to heal for a time then after an inspection, thrust back into the fiery furnace gradually getting closer to the final firing. The Creator just wants to burn off the impurities with the result that my brilliance will appear as dazzling as the beauty of gold.

God has provided this time of questions and His loving nurturing presence so that I may write. Why do I then fight and procrastinate? It is difficult to write my story because it causes me to relive the pain. It is easier for me to develop diversions like other work or my relationships. Those diversions bring the need for more and more of the same.

Again to quote *God Calling*, I read the following: "The longing of the human heart to be loved for itself is a something caught from the Great Divine Heart. Endurance is faith tried almost to the breaking point. The Divine Voice is not always expressed in words." It seems the Divine Voice we long to hear is heard through a heart-consciousness. It is more of an inner knowing. I note that in a race, it is not the start that hurts or even the pace of the long stretch. But it is when the goal is in sight that heart, nerves, courage and muscles are strained almost beyond human endurance, almost to the breaking point. That point is when we open to that inner voice. I offer the following advice on how to die to self: Give up the feeling that you are important to the process. You are part of the process but not the process, the process of reclaiming your Light—your Sight. Your Sight will come through your Light.

At this point I recall a dream that would sustain me during times when I felt as though I could not do anything to help myself. I call it the Brown Dog Dream. It began with me naked in a hospital-like corridor kneeling beside a large brown dog that was obviously male but was about to give birth. I was stroking the brown dog's head and making soothing sounds as the birthing process proceeded. As I looked around, I noticed others were there doing much the same as I. If they noticed I was naked, they gave no indication. Suddenly, I felt the need to go outside and I left. Outside, I encountered primal energies of darkness, fear and a foul substance that appeared to be feces. I found I was covered in the stench of it and sought the cleanliness and light of the birthing corridor. As I approached the big brown dog, I noticed a small brown puppy lying alongside. I was afraid to approach due to my shame; not only the shame of leaving when I was needed but also the condition of my body. But I was greeted by a warm loving look from both dogs and welcomed back in a loving embrace. The meaning of the dream is clear. The large brown dog is a representation of God and the self-birthing process. The little brown dog is me, the infant God-self. No matter that I run away to wallow in the muck of this life, the birthing process will continue with or without my presence. I will always be loved and welcomed back to the loving arms of the Creator.

As I've said earlier, when I receive information during a meditation, I have learned to act on it. This afternoon, I saw a name printed on a sign in my mind's eye. It is the name of a former client and also a close friend of one of my daughters. I don't understand why I need to speak with her but after dialing the phone number in Vermont, I know as soon as she answers the call. I am so shocked, I can barely speak but I manage to ask her, "Why? How could you do this?" A series of questions are flowing from my mouth and each one is repeated back to me as though she is a parrot. Suddenly, I realize why. He is there with her and she wants him to hear my side of the conversation. I begin to shake uncontrollably, as my husband comes to the phone. My anger and indignation rise to a crescendo. The final realization that my marriage has failed hits me like a brick.. I stand still for a few moments as the reality of my situation sinks in. A low moan begins deep within me rising from my bowels up through my throat and then becomes a scream. I move about as if in a dream as all the deceit of the past few months runs through my mind. My fear of the future begins to crawl over me as I cry. The terrible feelings of abandonment, of unworthiness, uselessness and of being unlovable all dance around me like ghouls from the grave pulling at my hair and clothing, pushing their ugly faces into mine where I can smell their foulness. In desperation, I summon a spark from deep within and my indignation flares like a full-fledged fire. I move swiftly around the house gathering his clothing, his stuff, old photos, whatever I can grab dragging it all outside where I stomp on it, and then burn what will burn. All the while I am screaming and crying. Had anyone witnessed my emotional outburst, they might have thought I had lost my mind but actually reacting as I have, has been very cleansing to my battered betrayed spirit. After the anger was spent, my mind is clear and I am better able to move ahead.

I realize after this phone call that I am probably the last person to know. In a well-meaning effort to spare me, they have decided to not tell me and that is why they have avoided talking with me. As it turns out, I am partially correct. One of my daughters knew but had been asked by my husband, not to tell me, on the pretext that he wanted to tell me himself. But he somehow hadn't gotten around to it. I discover, he has already moved into the other woman's house.

I call my daughters to explain what has happened. I want them to know the big secret is out in the open at last. They are angry and hurt. They feel they have been put in the middle of our dispute but are relieved to be able to discuss it openly. As I listen to them while they vent their anger and hurt, I realize a statement initially made in jest many years ago had actually become a reality. When my husband and I first agreed to marry, we used to say that he was marrying not one but four women because we came as a package deal. My son had chosen to live with his father at that time. I find my daughters are as wounded and hurt as I am. Their expression of anger is directed vocally towards their stepfather whereas mine is diffused by my intimate knowledge of the experience of the last three years of marital struggle. I also am able to work through a great deal of my pain and grief through my spiritual practice of meditation and by my physical distance.

I have hired a lawyer from North Carolina but within a few days, I am surprised by papers filing a suit against me in the Vermont court. I am now forced to appear in Vermont for the divorce action instead of North Carolina. I am hurt and angry because I feel this action was taken behind my back. It is easier for him to travel south than it is for me to travel north in my condition. The only other option I have is to file another separate action in North Carolina thereby paying for two attorneys. Since I don't see that second option as a possibility, I begin making calls to old friends in Vermont who will advise me on possible lawyers. I settle on a man in Vermont, who knows my husband but assures me that he would give me fair and nonprejudicial representation and will withdraw if he feels he is unable to do so.

I have made the decision to travel to Vermont for three months to visit my family and to meet with my lawyer and accountant. The challenge is finding someone to drive me and my pets up north. Most members of my family are committed to their jobs and unable to take time off to fly down to drive us northward. Finally, it is decided that one of my daughters will fly down in July, stay a couple of days then drive the pets and me back to Vermont. It seems like a long way off as the lonely days drag by.

I am basically an impatient person; always pushing for conclusions, results, answers and completion. I never did wait well and now even in my state of blindness, I find myself longing for time to pass quickly.

I remember as a child when I first began to experiment with Grandma's team of draft horses. They were named Duke and King but I took a fancy to Duke. I didn't plan for months to ride that horse, I just thought about it for a while and then one day spontaneously decided to do it. I had to drag a box over to his head to lift myself high enough to bridle him. I recall the weight of that heavy bridle with the blinders and heavy reins. The only riding equipment I had access to was used for harnessing the horses for driving. As I grew taller and stronger, I measured my growth by my ability to first of all carry the equipment and then later by being able to harness the horses by myself. It was several years before I was tall enough to jump on board without the aid of a fence, box or stump. Many times, if I fell off or had to dismount out on the trail somewhere, I walked home leading the horse, because I couldn't find a way to climb back on.

The first time I rode Duke was just like I had imagined it would be, a real life rodeo. After putting the bridle on, I led him out to the wooden gate. I led him in close parallel to the boards. Then I cautiously climbed up on the gate hoping he wouldn't move aside. Of course, he suspected something different was about to happen and therefore, moved his body out away from the gate. It took several attempts before I was able to make the leap and land squarely in the middle of that shiny broad back. It took only a second for him to realize that this was not the normal routine for him. He bolted away from the fence, hopping and bucking with me clinging as tight as I could with my short nine-year-old legs and my hands entwined in his long white mane. Around and around we went until he decided the best way to rid himself of the annoyance was to rub me off on the side of the barn. Having an eighteen-hundred-pound horse crushing my leg against a building was an effective way to get me off. I slid down over his wide rump to fall flat on my back in the dust. Still, I was exhilarated at having conquered the mighty beast. Well, kind of conquered anyway. There would be other days. It didn't take many tries before Duke and I were partners, covering many miles of hill and dale in all kinds of weather. It also was not too long before I had cut the blinders off the old harness bridle with my jackknife and braided myself some reins out of baling twine. Lucky for me, Grandma was preoccupied during this time and didn't notice the dismembered bridle for a long while.

Duke and I became unlikely playmates. We became a team that I felt could annialate anyone who attempted to accost us. There was a stretch of road near Grandma's farm where I had been approached by a young man on my way to see a friend. He grabbed me and attempted to pull me down in the bushes. He kept telling me to take my panties off. I was terrified and wrestled with him finally running as fast as I could down through the fields to my home. I didn't dare tell my mother about the incident because of her reaction from the other abuse I received at the hands of her Uncle. She wouldn't have believed me. Plus I was very ashamed. I was never able to walk that section of the road without fear until Duke became my partner and protector. On his broad back, I was able to travel that road and many others knowing we would get away fast.

We would go up into the piney woods and play hide and seek. After turning him loose, I would run behind a tree or a bush while he was munching on some grass. He would wheel around and eventually find me. Of course, I always had a treat for him in my jacket pocket. It got to the point where he would tear the pockets off my jacket to get those treats. My mother and grandmother became increasingly impatient with having to sew on my pockets. At one point in our little game, he grew weary and impatient with my childish ways and grabbed my arm tightly in his powerful teeth, then shook me. It was as though he was telling me, "Enough is enough, no more games." I learned quickly what my limitations were in my relationship with this large powerful friend.

In the nine years we spent together, he became one of my greatest teachers. One of the important lessons I learned from Duke was about unselfishly caring for another being. He taught me nurturing. Up to that time in my life I had never had to take care of any other living being but myself. There were small creatures in my life but not those that required my love and caring to the extent that Duke did. We had similar personalities in that we were always a bit rebellious and outside the ordinary. We also worked best when we worked alone. In a team situation, we were inclined to play and dance, share our joy, rather than just pull blindly and obediently forward.

Duke loved to run fast especially when I turned him towards home. The echo of his dinner-plate-size hooves on the road could be heard up through the valley. Many times as we crested the hill by Grandma's farm, she would be standing there, arms crossed sternly over her chest waiting in silence. After cooling him off, I would have to face a lecture on the proper deportment for young ladies and on proper horsemanship. Her lessons were tendered with gentleness however and I believe she understood the importance for me to act out my fantasies of being an Indian or a cowhand. When Grandma wasn't looking, Duke and I would ride out to the back pasture and chase the heifers around trying to lasso them as I had seen in the movies. Roping them was tricky because I was bareback and if I somehow managed to get a lucky shot with the rope, I was pulled off the horse and dragged around the field until I let go. This great old friend of mine lived to be thirty-five years old and was buried on the farm several years after I had married and moved to Vermont.

Fret not with that impatient hoof,
Snuff not the breezy wind,
The farther that thou fliest now,
So far am I behind.
EXCERPT FROM A POEM, *"THE ARAB'S FAREWELL TO HIS HORSE"*
BY CAROLINE NORTON

JUNE

To be alone and to be wise
Is a gift that comes
From the most natural
Called for
Difficult birthing of Self.

EXCERPT FROM A POEM
BY MARGUERITE ESTANALEHI BARTLEY

After spending a great deal of time indoors because of the strong light of summer, I feel I am losing my connection to the earth. I don't go out in the yard even after the sun goes down; because the density of mosquitoes drives me back inside. Since I spend so much time quite high above the surface of the earth, I make a conscious effort to ground in the earth's energy by going out in the yard to meditate. I have a vision of walking out into a beautiful garden. There are fountains and beautiful flowers everywhere. As I approach the steps to climb back upstairs to my home, I notice a cavern under the bottom step. I bend down to peer into the depths of the darkness visible only by a thin shaft of light. As I step back from the cavern, a pair of hands in the prayer position extend out through the opening. An almost overwhelming feeling of sadness emanates from the small crevice. This, I believe, is a plea from the Earth Mother begging me to connect with her energy. A second dream a day later reveals that I want to fly out of here but as

I approach the runway to taxi out, I realize there is a vibration in the engines. I shut them down. The thunder and lightning are all around me. Then it is too late; I am needed right here on the ground. After the confirmation of the second dream, I am making an effort to sit in the garden as much as possible focusing on bringing the earth energy into my body through my root chakra. The root or base chakra is located between the legs and connects with the coccyx or tailbone. It is the first chakra of our energy system. This is the area where we energetically direct our fight/flight response. If we are not fully grounded through this chakra, we may suffer from mental illness or physical illnesses such as diseases of the spinal column, legs, bones, feet, rectum and immune system. When we are not grounded through this chakra, we tend to feel frightened, alone and isolated. We feel unattached and disconnected from life and those around us.

My feelings at this time: The ones I love the most are abandoning me, attacking me, and judging me or just plain ignoring me. It seems everything is being taken from me. There is nothing left for me here. I feel destitute. Yea, though I walk through the valley of the shadow of death, I will fear no evil. These feelings are all originating from my ungrounded state. Each day I work through these endless thoughts of abandonment and despair. I have come to realize my children are feeling the very same feelings as I. I have decided to give them space to adjust and resolve their fears in their own way. Even as I struggle with the feeling that I have totally botched this life, I feel the earth under my feet and I continue to reach up, call out and lift my eyes, surrendering to the strength of the arms that will safely pull me up. Today, as I cry in despair, Earth Mother weeps with me. We are being drenched in refreshing rain.

During a meditation, I am visited by a presence who introduces himself as a great-grandfather named Dorian. He is English and often appears in a long overcoat and brown trousers. He is tall, thin and has a shock of thick black hair. As I sit in my garden by the water, I feel the warmth and friendship of Dorian. I am surprised and pleased to feel his strong hands on my shoulders. There is love and caring in his touch. The air is crisp and clear, sunny and bright. It feels quiet and cool, beautiful; I thank God. Sometimes our greatest fears are met and cleared by calling out in love for help.

A former neighbor called me today from Vermont and has offered her townhouse to me for the month of July. I look upon it as a gift—God has given me the time to acclimate to being back in the family energy; a quiet time to process the real purpose of my visit in this blind and disabled state. I plan to spend a week or so with each one of my children. I also plan to visit my sister for a while and my friend, Nicky in Massachusetts. The visit will culminate in the wedding of my stepdaughter in Rhode Island in September.

Shortly after receiving the divorce papers the first week of this month, I had the following dream: I stand outside the old one room school house where I spent the first six years of my early education. Now there is a wing on each side of the one big center room. The wings are burning down as I watch from the yard with my husband and his girlfriend. Great waves of sadness engulf me. They are standing there looking very smug as they turn and speak to me, "Look, our section, the main one, doesn't burn." Then, as if on cue, it too catches and burns. They are saddened too.

With self-pride comes a separation from God. When those feelings come in, I need to call on God's guiding hand. I need to remember E.G.O., which is an acronym for "Edging God Out". Often, I am still confronted with the feeling that I have failed God somehow and have been cast from grace. My ego kicks in and builds on those feelings, pushing out all feelings of love, compassion and service. Yet, when I am with other healers or like-minded people, I remember standing in my place of power before this dis-ease. I focus on letting go of self, dying to self as God only works through the humble and the weak. Now I am weak and sick, therefore it is time to release those old thought forms which originate in the ego. God has given me the gift of being a channel of energetic healing. As my ego would have it, it was not enough that I was a beautiful child of God. No, I had to be better and brighter than anyone else. My ego wanted to be in control. I wanted to make me special. How foolish of me. God is opening me and using me in many powerful ways of service. I am grateful for these insights into self. I will continue to pray on the emptying of ego-self thoughts. I am not sure where I fit into the grand scheme of things but I know I must be clear to find out. "Be still and know that I am God", my Creator instructs. I am being given the gift of sight. I must have insight to gain out sight.

A friend from New Bern asks me to attend a sweat lodge ceremony near her home. The ceremony was organized about a year ago by a small group of devotees. The turtle-like dome is located in the backyard of the leader of the group. They meet once a month to sit in circle, pray and sweat together. I have participated one other time in a similar ceremony. I am familiar with the protocol and ritual. I know the heat will not make my eyes any worse. Actually, it will probably help by cleansing many of the toxins out of my body. I am acutely aware of the diagnosis given by a doctor in Raleigh of the possibility that I suffer from heavy metal poisoning caused by years of carelessness in the handling of toxins on the farm and in my oil painting. I recall as a child I helped my father in his garage as he repaired engines. My child hands and arms were thrust up to the elbows in a vat of gasoline as I scrubbed pistons with a wire brush. Many of those metals can be released through the sweat glands and the urinary tract. The heat and steam in the lodge could possibly help to rid my body of these toxic substances. The sweat lodge is one of several sacred ceremonies the Native Americans have shared with us through multi-racial teaching groups such as the Bear Tribe formed by Sun Bear, a Chippewa Medicine Teacher. The entire process of building the lodge, gathering the wood, the stones, lighting the fire and the fasting preparation for going into the lodge as well as the actual sweating in the lodge is sacred. The lodge itself is constructed of bent saplings bound together to form a dome-like structure that resembles a turtle. The harvesting of the saplings is completed in sacred respect for the trees that give their lives for our benefit. Building the lodge is a magical experience. The saplings are sometimes two inches or more in diameter. They are sharpened on one end and pushed into the earth with blessings of tobacco and cornmeal. Then using a bracing technique, the resistant saplings are stroked and rubbed by many hands until they bend and conform to the desired shape. They are lashed one to another to form the turtle shape. A fire pit is built outside in the East. Stones are gathered and placed on a carefully arranged grid-work of firewood. Each stone is offered with a prayer. Then the wood is arranged to cover all the stones. The fire is lit and will be tended throughout the ceremony by a fire tender. When the stones are hot, they are swept clean of any residue of ashes that might smoke up the lodge. Then, they are brought into the lodge by a member who has volunteered to be a stone carrier. Inside the lodge a pit is dug in the earth where the hot stones are laid. Fragrant, healing herbs are sprinkled on the stones. Water is poured over the hot stones causing great plumes of steam to arise, cleansing and carrying the prayers of the people upward to Great Spirit. Additional stones are brought in during the four rounds of prayers. The four rounds represent the four directions of the winds.

The early Americans referred to this continent as turtle island. The reference is clear in the shape of the lodge. It is with deep reverence and trust that I bend to place my forehead on Earth Mother as I crawl symbolically back into her womb this evening. During the lodge ceremony, the great grizzly bear appears before me and I am given an insight into why this total transformation is happening to me. It is clear to me that my mission is now to separate from my marital relationship. Then, to devote my entire life, to the group effort of raising the consciousness and energy of this mass of humanity to enable us all to ascend orderly, gently and with as little chaos and destruction as possible. Many of us are now called. My life is about feeling my sense of value on the planet by the amount and kind of work I do for others. It is all about love and service. I must be grounded on this earth plane solidly to do this work. I will be cleared to see now, perhaps not physically but certainly energetically, to do the work of the Creator God. I continue to pray for all those who are blind in any way to the Light that God offers in abundance.

Today, the humidity has built up and waves of heat can be seen rising from the earth. The air is heavy and hot, distant thunder rumbles. As I glance to the west, I notice the ominous darkness of the sky and observe by the trees that the wind had changed direction. We will have rain soon. I manage to cover the porch furniture and batten things down as best I can in preparation for the storm. One needs to be prepared in this coastal area. Powerful winds, hail and heavy rain quite often accompany storms here along the Neuse River and Pamlico Sound. Tornado watches and warnings are common occurrences during the spring and summer months. I check the computer radar weather station and see that we are in the path of some very severe thundershowers. Duffy and Pumpkin beg to come inside. They know when there is danger long before we humans do. I check the weather every few minutes. Just as I reach the sink for a drink of water, I feel a shudder go through the house as the first blast of wind strikes. The thought occurs to me to collect my four-legged friends and go to the basement room where I keep a cot set up for just such emergencies. As I glance toward the creek, a second more powerful blast hits bringing the rain. I briefly have time to see my aluminum johnboat with motor and still tied to the dock, fly into the air. The rain is horizontal and so heavy that it makes visibility difficult but I see enough to warrant the grabbing of both pets while scrambling to the basement shelter. As we huddle here, I hear unfamiliar noises coming from above our heads as the house absorbs the force of wind and rain. Although, time seems to stand still, the storm only lasts a few minutes. We venture tentatively back upstairs to check for damage. I am surprised to find a large puddle of water on the wooden floor of the living room. Apparently, the clerestory windows were not locked and the force of the wind drove the rain underneath. Outside there is a path of destruction. Bushes, trees and my aluminum boat are victims of what appear to have been straight-line winds. Clearly the storm went through the nearby woods then struck a little settlement to the east before going out into the sound. I have lost my motor to the damaging salt water but the boat is unharmed.

One of the big red-tipped bushes that was knocked down holds a mockingbird nest with three babies barely hatched. The parents are circling and calling in distress as I make my way carefully down the front steps. It is still raining lightly but the coolness is refreshing. As I poke my head into the foliage, there are the babes still nestled safely in the nest, wet but none the worse for wear. I want to try to save the bushes and leave the nest intact. I gather rope and wooden boards for braces. The roots are not completely out of the earth so it seems like they might survive if I can get them upright and braced. The bushes are easily ten feet tall and nearly as big around but I manage to get one of them up just as my neighbor drives in to check on me. With his help, the bushes and the mockingbird nest survive.

I wonder what impact the storm has had on the baby birds after they were flung to the earth. I keep an eye on them from the window upstairs for a few days. Now, I watch as two young mockingbirds take their first short flights from the nest to the lawn. Within a couple of hours, they are flying around like experienced pilots. The one remaining bird however has a different idea. It calls plaintively, "weep, weep, weep" to its parents who are sympathetic to the youngster's fear of leaving the nest. As I watch, they encourage and plead with the fearful bird, asking it to make the leap of faith but it just cannot bring itself to do it. The wretched bird climbs out of the nest and eases its way to the end of the branch but still is unable to spread wings and fly in trust and faith. Toward the end of the day in its still fearful state, it climbs back into the nest for the night. I notice the parents continue to feed and support their reluctant offspring throughout the process. The same scenario is repeated for two more days. The third day, which somehow seems appropriate to me, the fledgling, leaps and flies to the ground. I'll bet it closed its eyes but it has done it and before long it is zooming around the yard with its siblings. I realize that the whole storm story including the reluctance of the mockingbird to make the leap of faith is a metaphor for my journey in this life.

"The attainment of wholeness requires one to stake one's whole being. Nothing less will do; there can be no easier conditions, no substitutes, no compromises."

CARL JUNG

JULY

Time present and time past
Are both perhaps present in time future,
And time future contained in time past.
EXCERPT FROM *BURNT NORTON* BY T.S.ELIOT

The days are hot and steamy. Time seems endless as each day blends into another. I have been fascinated with time for much of my life and now I struggle with the mystery of why the days seem to pass quickly even though I am not working or doing much of anything other than a few routine tasks.

I feel I have moved to that point of timelessness, a still point perhaps where the deepest form of healing takes place. This is a place of complete surrender and vulnerability; a place of peace. Elliot goes on in part to say in part II of his poem, "Burnt Norton":

And the outer compulsion, yet surrounded
By a grace of sense, a white light still and moving . . . .

I am aware of being surrounded by white light. I surrender to that light and am guided inward to a place of contentment and joy. I have, at last, begun to heal. The rebirthing process has commenced.

The fourth of July in this part of North Carolina is celebrated with unusual gusto. After ten years of comings and goings, I am at last going to be able to be part of the famed celebration. In Oriental, it is known as the Croaker Festival. The word "Croaker" is the name of a fish that makes a croaking sound when it is caught. The croakers are plentiful in the surrounding waters this time of the year. The Croaker Festival has become a three-day event featuring music, street dances, food booths, crafts and a down-home type of parade extravaganza. The event culminates in a firework display set off of Teaches Point. Local legend has it that the old oak tree still standing on the point was a place where Edward Teach, also known as Blackbeard, once stationed a lookout as he skillfully hid his loot—filled pirate ships in our secluded waters. I am eager to immerse myself in at least some of the celebration. A neighbor has offered to take me to the parade. The day has dawned hot and humid. We position ourselves at a vantage point along the street and sit down on the curbside to wait for the first glimpse of the parade.

As I sit here with the bill of my baseball cap pulled down, eyes closed, covered with dark glasses, I travel back in time to a Fourth of July celebration forty-six years earlier in Pittstown, New York, where I grew up. I had been riding Grandma's 1800 lb. draft horse Duke for a couple of years and wanted to participate in the annual parade with several other riders. Of course, I didn't have any tack and rode by the seat of my pants, literally. I decided I would appear as an Indian and spoke to Grandma about it. She was reluctant at first to allow me to take Duke out in a crowd such as there was sure to be but as time passed and I begged, she consented. I scrubbed and curried Duke's white hide until it shone like white satin. I shampooed and braided his long white mane and tail, and trimmed his fetlocks close to his legs. He did look handsome and he seemed to sense something special was about to occur. On the morning of the parade, I dressed in shorts and a T-shirt with bare feet. Actually, that was my daily attire for the summer. I still envisioned myself an Indian even though I didn't have an actual costume. I certainly carried the proper spirit within me. Early in the morning on the Fourth, I rode down to the place designated for the start of the parade. There was a committee person lining up the marching bands, the fire trucks, floats, and the half dozen or so horses and riders. Duke was nervous and danced around turning in circles. He seemed to be wound tight like a spring about to burst forth and unwind. In my eleven-year-old mind, I thought it was great to have him prancing and dancing about. He was a symbol of my fiery spirit as well. Finally, they had us all lined up and the bands began to play. The bands played very loud and they were very close to us. We moved slowly down the street for about five hundred feet as the drums reached a crescendo of pulsing beat. Duke's nervous system could not take any more of the chaotic sounds that accompany a parade. He stood high on his hind legs and began to walk down the road in that position. There were people lining the sides of the road. I was not able to control him much during his two-legged walk. Bystanders began to clap and cheer as they misunderstood our performance. I yelled for them to stay back because I wasn't sure where we were going. As we neared the turn to Grandma's, he decided he was going back to the safety of his barn no matter what stood in his way. As it turned out the only thing standing in his way to his goal was a car. Duke bolted, leaped clean over the hood of the car then taking the bit in his teeth, galloped home. That was the one and only parade I ever undertook with a horse. It certainly was a major teaching lesson for me. I was humbled by the lack of control I had over the horse and was ashamed to show my face in that group of riders for months after. Duke and I became a kind of local curiosity as time went on because of our escapades in and around town. We presented quite a picture as we galloped headlong up and down the streets. His huge rubber-shod hooves created an echo that could be heard all down the valley. I often rode clad only in a bathing suit. My feet were bare and my hair cropped very short. I did resemble the native people that I felt so close to as my body browned in the sun. Duke and I became fast friends and displayed our fiery natures more times than I like to admit.

Now I am peering out from squinted eyes trying to see the various floats as they pass by. But as the horses pass, I can still feel in my legs the life and vibration of that giant white horse rearing and plunging along in time to the pounding drums.

After the Croaker Festival parade, my friend and I tour the exhibits. She leads me by the hand but I can see very little and it is crowded so we, too, gallop home. That evening, I am picked up by another neighbor and taken over to their dock in Whortonsville to watch the fireworks.

Actually, it wasn't watch as much as listen to the fireworks for me but it was fun to be with others celebrating another Independence Day.

It is the second week in July; my daughter has come down and will spend a couple of days before we pack the car with my gear and my four-legged friends for the drive northward. Both of my animals have traveled a great deal and therefore travel easily. We divide the trip into two days and it is quite pleasant and uneventful. After all, it is unusual and pleasant to spend time alone with a grown daughter who normally is surrounded by three young sons. I treasure these gifts of quiet sharing.

Perhaps it is a mistake to think that I can go back to the same townhouse complex where I had lived for ten years with my husband. But at the time I accepted the offer I felt I needed a place to readjust gradually before being immersed in the family dynamics. The townhouse that was so graciously loaned to me for three weeks adjoins the townhouse that had been ours. My pets are thrilled beyond reason when they realize where they are, especially the old cat, Pumpkin. He has patrolled all the old haunts of his youth. It isn't too long, however, before his sixteen year old body catches up with that youthful spurt of energy and he tires to the point of collapse. After two weeks in Vermont, he has refused to eat and lies on a blanket prepared to die. I sit with him for long periods of time, rubbing him gently all the while encouraging him to do whatever he needs to do. I am fully prepared for his departure from this world. I have communicated with the vet regarding his symptoms and the state of his health. We have decided to not take any heroic measures, as it seems to be a complete failure of his inner organs. After of week of being in a place where he has teetered between life and death, I have to make a decision. I am supposed to leave the townhouse and move in with my oldest daughter. As it turns out, she is renting a house and pets are prohibited. Reluctantly, I will take Pumpkin to the vet's kennel. They have promised to keep me posted on his condition and to not treat him except for dehydration. I call each day fully expecting to be told that he has died but after the third day, he has begun to eat and drink once again.

His rebirth and resurrection are very symbolic for me. After the first week of excitement of having returned to Vermont, my fragile spirit has crashed and I feel like I, too, am going to die. All the feelings of despair, abandonment and the pain I had experienced earlier in my process have returned with such force I can barely breathe. I don't recall ever being in such a place of deep despair except perhaps after the birth of my fourth child when I suffered from postpartum depression. The main difference is the fear that surrounded that depression of my youth. This time I am not afraid because I no longer fear death or separation. My responsibilities are only for my pets and myself now; I don't have four young children to care for. I now understand what is happening to me but none-the-less, it is an incredible experience of nearly intolerable pain. I have to go down into the spiritual darkness of my psyche and own it. I didn't know I had such darkness in me. Since I have been in the light, it is amazing to feel this kind of human destructive force. It has expressed itself in rage from time to time. I erupted in rage when I discovered that my husband was living with another woman early in the spring but now all I feel, is a profound sadness.

Early in my youth, my older sister took me with her on dates. I believe my mother must have asked her to be responsible for me. I was three and a half years younger than she. I followed her and her friends in and out of bars around our area, posing as a legal drinker. Her friends took me under their wings and proceeded to teach me how to drink like a grown up. I was a willing student but not very adaptable. Usually I became very ill and developed terrible hangovers. I was a rather shy teenager with a very low self-esteem. I read every book in the school library on how to make people like me. I felt left out and different from the other kids my age. They always seemed to be so cool, so popular and pretty. My self-image was very low. I was tall, thin and large breasted. I never got carded for my illegal drinking because I always looked eighteen. I started with screwdrivers, and then tried sloe gin fizzes. I hated the taste of beer so I couldn't get that past my nose. But the effect the alcohol had on my self-esteem was not lost on me. After the first two drinks I became the most beautiful, popular girl in the bar. I flirted with all of my sister's boyfriends, danced on tabletops, made people laugh, and became the child prodigy of the partying set. Then I met my future husband when I was fourteen; he was twenty-one and had just mustered out of the navy. He instructed me to drink scotch straight up and promised I would not become ill. I practiced and practiced but still I would become sick after two or three drinks. No one in my family ever drank so my education in these matters was kept secret. Then later on after my children were born, I had my first blackout. I became very frightened and ashamed deciding never to drink again but soon I was back at it again. I was working in Manchester, Vermont, in real estate when my drinking became an acceptable way of life. For the first time, I was drinking during the day at lunch, then later in the afternoon with friends. One night two friends and I decided to celebrate a sale one of us had made, so we went out for drinks right after work. I don't remember anything of that evening and I was doing the driving. I awoke at home, in my bed, with a terrible hangover. My husband stood over me waving a charcoal-broiled steak wrapped in aluminum foil that he found in my car along with the stench of alcohol. I don't have a clue what I did that night. All I know is that for a period of six hours or so I was out driving and drinking with a male colleague. The experience really sobered me and I stopped drinking at that point. Over the years, occasionally I would have a drink or two but I kept it in check until I married my second husband. I tried to keep pace with his drinking. He encouraged me to drink champagne because I became such a comic. There were many horrible scenes between us due to our drinking. Alcohol made him angry and it enabled me to fight back. There was at least one more black-out drunk for me before I gave up the use of alcohol totally. By the grace of God, I was not addicted for life. The old training comes back now as I feel unable to cope. I settle in with a bottle of good red wine. Two glasses later, I am sick and dizzy, feeling worse than I did before I took the wine. I believe Pumpkin picked up on my emotional state of mind and prepared to die. As soon as he was away from my energy and surrounded by the busy activities of the kennel, he recovered with miraculous speed.

My daughter has moved me down to her house after we deposited Pumpkin and Duffy dog in the kennel. She and her husband have planned a camping trip in the Mohawk River basin of New York State. My two grandchildren are considerate of my handicap. They each want to take my hand to guide me around. They are careful to tell me when there is a step or a curb. Initially, I was quite hesitant to walk with any assurance as I have taken several bad falls not only by myself but also while being guided by others who forgot to warn me of pitfalls. It isn't long before I realize the children are more attentive and reliable than the adults. Now upon my return, I am gradually beginning to feel connected once again to my family as we share this special adventure. I feel like a stranger meeting them for the first time. They didn't know me in my singleness or in my dependant state. My role as matriarch/leader does not exist any longer. We dance around each other trying to figure out our new roles and how to play them. I note some resentment from my children. One daughter is quite clear about the reason she feels it. She says that she had not planned on having a single dependant parent to care for at this stage of her life. She always thought we, my husband and I, would care for one another for many more years until one of us died or became ill requiring our children to care for us. I appreciate her honesty and candidness. Actually, it has not occurred to me to ask any of my children to come to my aid. I am doing fine on my own in North Carolina with the help of my neighbors and friends. I still cling to the belief that since my body has decided to accept this eye condition that it can also make the decision to let go of it. Since I don't know if I have Sjogrens, I feel certain my eye challenge will clear up as soon as the divorce is final and the stress surrounding it has been eliminated. I do not see myself as permanently disabled.

There is still the question of why I have this disease. Apart from all the metaphysical reasons, which I have explored and am still exploring today, I am attempting to find a physical reason hidden in there somewhere. Earlier in the year a physician in Raleigh had evaluated me. The diagnosis was heavy metal poisoning especially mercury and lead. In my early childhood, I was exposed many times to lead-based products and gasoline as well as fertilizers and pesticides. Being an oil painter for thirty-five years would have exposed me to more heavy metals. Then in 1980, there was the apparent fish-poisoning incident in the Virgin Islands.

I know I have to take charge of my own health and treatment. So I continue to seek answers not only from the allopathic side of medicine but from the alternative or integrative side. Polarity energy balancing treatments offer me immediate relief but I am unable to receive them with the frequency needed. Acupuncture and Chinese herbs offer some relief especially for the accompanying dry eye but again I am faced with a formidable expense due to the frequency and number of treatments necessary. It is unfortunate that the insurance companies don't see the need to cover preventative and integrative care.

It seems very likely that what I am currently experiencing could indeed be caused by my exposure to heavy metals. One of the ways to cleanse the body tissues of the poisons is through EDTA Chelation Therapy. A neighbor gave me the name of a doctor who would give the EDTA I.V. therapy. The definition of 'chelation' is a grabber—literally. The word is derived from the Greek 'chele' and refers to the claw of a crab or lobster. A substance is 'chelated' out of the body when it is grabbed, trapped and transformed by a chelating agent.

Ethylene diamine tetra-acetic acid (EDTA) is a man-made amino acid chelating agent with a particular affinity for toxic metals such as lead, mercury, cadmium and aluminum. Should EDTA meet up with such toxic substances, the material is sequestered, and then secreted in bodily wastes. The Environmental Physicians have proven in their research that when the body is rid of toxic metals it is better able to return to health. EDTA is administered through a series of intravenous drips over the course of several months.

The doctor is in Massachusetts, a three and one-half hour drive away. He recommends that I receive ten treatments besides a mineral and vitamin C injection from time to time as the EDTA also removes minerals and vitamin C from the system. It is difficult finding drivers to take me the to the treatment center twice a week besides being very expensive. EDTA therapy is not covered by insurance. My joints and muscles did feel better than they had since 1980. I manage to have five treatments before my stay in Vermont comes to a close and I return south.

Looking at the prospect of visiting all four of my grown children and their families over the course of the summer will certainly be a learning experience for all of us. Very rarely does a parent get to live with each family consecutively as a single parent. My family seems to be gathering around and unifying once again. They have been in the thick of our break up geographically. It is challenging to live in a small community when a prominent couple as we were end their long–term marriage.

I am being given an incredible opportunity for soul growth through this entire process. The soul doesn't always grow in all positive lessons but it grows through the entire human experience. I have experienced all three poles of this life, the positive, the negative and the neutral. By balancing the two opposite forces within the neutral place, I have left the pain and despair behind to arrive at a place of peace.

Even if this blindness does not disappear, I believe that I will be able to go on with my life in a constructive manner and still manage to do the work that God has asked me to do. I have enjoyed excellent sight for much of my life. I have taught people in my painting classes to see. To see all the vastness of this world, to see all there is out there for them and to see the connectedness of it all. I taught them to observe subtle shades, values, lights and shadows. I showed them how to apply the lessons to their lives. I will continue to teach but in a different way. I know I have been given a ministry but I am not certain yet how it will unfold. I am being given many gifts of insight. Much of my current blindness has involved the gathering of insights rather than outsight. As my insight becomes clearer, I become more detached from being a mother/matriarch to being a loving witness who realizes what is and what is not hers to do. I am finally able to give up the control issues I have with my children. Another "D" word lesson in detachment.

I died from minerality and became vegetable;
And from vegetativeness I died and became animal.
I died from animality and became man.
Then why fear disappearance through death?
Next time I shall die
Bringing forth wings and feathers like angels;
After that, soaring higher than angels-
What you cannot imagine,
I shall be that.

JELALUDDIN RUMI

AUGUST

A cover of darkness, separation, and confusion are necessary prerequisites for the eventual rebirth of a lost and wandering soul.
EXCERPT FROM *"THE MOON AND THE GODDESS"* BY NOR HALL

I am greeted by a dream of great significance the first week of August. I stand on a mountain pinnacle. An inn owned by an old man is located there. The sides are steep so that everything falls away into the vastness of space. My husband and others are with me. We are hungry and ask for food. The ancient innkeeper provides. The others don't want to eat his food, as he looks rather old and dirty. I don't really notice and I am unafraid. I eat fully and feel very joyous. My friend has eaten a bit and has stomach cramps. She blames the food. I sleep in a small room with my husband but it is unpleasant because of bright lights and the loud music he has chosen. I defiantly shut off the lights and music and leave the room. I am presented with a beautiful box of huge pale peach colored fragrant roses that are exquisite in form and fragrance. I note however, that the stems are all cut short. In the next second, I am in the bathroom with my husband. Suddenly a mysterious shower sprays down on us. I run out the door to complain to the manager of the inn but he just laughs. The inn has suddenly gotten much larger and more elegant. People I haven't seen for a long while recognize me and wave. A handicapped woman I had known before tells me how happy she is to see me. She walks back inside with me to eat. People dressed in black are sleeping all over lobby. In my room, which is lovely and has a spectacular view, is a feast spread before me. I share it with my friends.

I feel this dream expresses my ability to move on in strength and beauty. The connection with my feminine self is positive and strong. I have the support of many old friends and I look forward to meeting new ones. My life will be a feast of new ideas, nourishment and sharing. I am feeling stronger and more confident as I begin my journey from family to family for the next two months.

Pumpkin is doing so well being cared for by the people at the kennel that I decide to leave him there until I move to my sister's home in New York, later in the month. Once there, he can roam around the yard safely. Duffy and I are currently staying at my son's home for the next week or so. We are sleeping in the camper out in the yard because they don't have a guest room. I enjoy staying out in the camper because it provides me some privacy and it is easier with the dog. My daughter-in-law is very kind and loving. She extends her grace and compassion with an offer to open their home to me on a full time basis if I needed that level of care. I feel welcome and loved. However, I want deeply to sit with my son to discuss our shared pain and differences. Each morning he waves to me as he drives by the camper on his way to work. At night we meet at the dinner table but the opportunity to speak on the level I desire are just not available. The veils between us prevent our sharing any intimate conversation. I lack the strength to determine if it is the right time to initiate such a conversation. I feel separate and detached from my son during this visit.

During my stay in my son's family, I do share some special moments with my five-year-old granddaughter. It seems as though much of this visit to my family in the north is about bonding with my grandchildren. She inquired if she could stay with me in the camper one night. As we settled down in the double bed together and after reading several books, (she read to me), she began to ask many questions mostly about death and dying. Their family had just lost a close friend to cancer and death was fresh in her mind. I answered her questions as clearly and honestly as I could. Then she asked where Jesus lived. I explained that Jesus lives in our hearts. She was quiet for a time. Suddenly, she rose up on one elbow and looking down in my face; she said she didn't want Jesus living in her heart because there wasn't enough room in there for him. She has persisted throughout my visit to attempt to "counsel" me regarding my marital state of affairs. She is obviously struggling with the fact that her grandparents are no longer living together. Through her eyes life is simply about forgiving and loving. Oh, if we could just keep it that simple and live by the ideals of a child.

Twice now during my stay in the camper, I have bumped my head, my eye and the side of my nose hard on the braces that support the awning over the door. Each time I have blackened my eye and bruised my nose, I have cried out in frustration and pain. "Now we have reached the point of physical mutilation. What do you want from me? Must I bleed? What else can I do," I sobbed. No obvious answers have been received but I do proceed with more humility and caution.

My next visit is with another daughter on Lake Bomoseen and then on to my sister's for a short time. I will also spend some time with my third daughter in Albany. I have made an appointment with an ophthalmologist in Rutland who has previously looked after my eyes. He appears horrified as I am helped into his office. He immediately suggested I go to one of the big three eye centers on the East Coast. I chose Boston and the referral is been made. My successes with the doctors I have seen up to this point have left me less than enthusiastic or optimistic about seeing another one.

Meanwhile, moving around from house to house, living out of my suitcase and my car is taking a great energy toll on me. I shudder when I think of how many times I have blindly unpacked and repacked that suitcase and how many times I dragged my stuff out to the trunk of the car and back again. My car has become a moveable closet. It has been moved with me and therefore is accessible for storage. During this time I have been spending in Vermont, near my husband's offices, I have gone in several times to sort through our things that are stored there in the apartment that was once to be our temporary home together. I somehow get through those trips by drawing on some inner reserves. I try to plan the trips so I will not accidentally run into my husband. But today when my daughter and I went into his office to download my computer files to discs, he was there and insisted on helping me. Sitting very closely to me, he began to choose the files that he thought I wanted to take with me. I could feel his eyes and his presence very strongly. He appeared to be loving and kind. His demeanor shocked my daughter and she remarked about the apparent feelings he still felt for me when we finally escaped. Neither of us could understand how he was living with another woman while still obviously caring for me. I feel drained and in a great deal of pain now after our meeting.

The apartment is upstairs and is without air conditioning. I suffer from the excessive heat even though I deliberately came as early in the morning as possible. Going through old photos and letters is the most painful process. This all just seems unreal to me. I feel like I am moving through a fog and numbness has taken over my senses. It is, like I said before, a very bad dream.

Silently, I pray to return home. Even though family members surround me, the history of my life for the last twenty-six years is all around me. It is oppressive and I feel suffocated. My family is busy with their schedules and I am alone nearly every day during the week. It affords me time to think and absorb the weight of the sadness that has permeated every home I have visited. Some friends from North Carolina have apparently picked up on my prayers. They call and ask if I want them to drive to Vermont to bring me back home.

I am able to visit with my mom while staying at my sister's house and also to spring Pumpkin from the kennel. He seems revitalized and enjoys being at my sister's. I think he feels he has become a resident at a fancy retirement home for cats. She pampers him and loves him; he just soaks it all up and heals, as do I.

My sister and mother take me shopping today for clothing. I cannot remember the last time I have been shopping for myself. I have lost a great deal of weight and most of the things I brought with me don't fit properly. We load ourselves with possibilities and all pile into the changing room together like a trio of teenagers. I model while they make various comments, sometimes giggling and sometimes downright belly-laughing. The experience is very uplifting for me. After a sumptuous lunch at a local café, we top off the day with a pedicure and haircut. I feel like a new woman in my tight black jeans, T-shirt and high-heeled boots. I gratefully accept their love and support.

During my stay in Albany with my daughter and her family, she drives me to Boston to see the opthalmologist. We stay all night in Marblehead with her sister-in-law and then return the next afternoon. As we sit in the doctor's posh office, the thought foremost in my mind is, what a waste of time and money. I don't have any medical coverage at this time so it will come straight out of pocket. Lying around on end tables are large impressive textbooks authored by the doctor I am to see. Dollar signs take over my mind. They start the process of examining me and gathering my history by sending me from one to another underling like an assembly line. Finally, at the end of the line, is the big guy, the king, the big cheese. You get a few minutes with him while he looks over what all his employees have done along the line. He basically said he couldn't see any reason why my eyes were not opening. I am just about to walk out the door when I turn to him and said, "Why is it my eyes won't open in the dark?" He seemed astounded at my question. His comment was, "If that is the case, then I think I know what you have. You have Benign Essential Blepharospasm." He went on to explain briefly that BEB was a type of dystonia and manifested as involuntary spasms of the eye lids. Now we are getting somewhere. Finally after a year of searching, I finally have a diagnosis—albeit a tentative one but a diagnosis none-the-less. The Boston doctor urges me to seek treatment here but I am going back south shortly. I am given the names of some doctors at the University of North Carolina, Chapel Hill, but I won't be able to see them until October. I often think what would have happened if I hadn't blurted out my question in frustrated anger that day. How many more doctors would I have been passed on to? It appears it was time for answers.

August 10th marks the first anniversary of my dad's passing. I am spending the day with my sister and family. We share a wonderful picnic reunion in the out-of-doors. He loved those picnics. He loved the clams baked on the outdoor barbecue. Dad truly enjoyed being with his family in celebration of any event. In earlier times, he would host clambakes and picnics, always providing more food than we could possibly eat. I miss my dad even though he had been in a nursing home for the last two years of his life. I still could call him on the phone or go visit him when I was in the north. It seems funny when he was a younger man, he never liked to talk on the phone but as he came to be an old man, he enjoyed our conversations. For most of my life, I yearned to hear him say he loved me but it wasn't until one of our telephone calls that he finally said it to me. I was overwhelmed—such a seemingly insignificant thing but so powerful for me. I knew he loved me but I needed to hear it from his lips as the words flowed from his heart. I never had a letter from my dad. He didn't write much down and his spelling was pretty bad. He never completed school because of his father's illness. He was needed on the farm to keep it going. He had a good mind and much potential but he never complained about his lot in life. He lived his later years with grace and dignity as my mother does today. The early years were tough on my parents. They worked hard to provide for us but money was always an issue in those days especially with four children to care for. He was tense and angry much of the time. We all walked on eggs for fear of setting him off. His rage was always vented on my mother, never on us. He behaved like a drinking man but he was not. My father could fix anything from automobiles to electrical wiring. He built our home, then my sister's home and also helped with my first house.

My first home, not house, was a 30' x 8' aluminum trailer. We borrowed it rent-free from my husband's brother. As a very young bride, it appealed to me as a playhouse. I did not live in the real world back then. I was finally going to escape from my parent's home where I was always considered the different one, the odd one, to my very own little house almost two hours away. My perception of the little dollhouse changed to that of a prison that first winter as I lay in bed suffering from morning sickness that was exacerbated by loneliness and homesickness. It was a particularly brutal winter that year. The windows frosted over completely with thick ice blocking out all but a dim light from the sun. We struggled to keep warm and to keep the water pipes from freezing solid. The floors were cold—the blankets froze to the floors during the night. It was as though we were living in a refrigerator. But we survived and in July I gave birth to my first child, a son. I was filled with awe and wonder at the perfect being I had helped to create. My prior experience at child rearing was minimal. I was too frightened as a youngster to baby-sit for others as my older sister did. I did not have a clue as to how to feed, bathe or change that child. My mother came for a few days but she was still working full time and could not take time from her job. She got me started and then my cousin came. My cousin had some experience helping with younger siblings but knew nothing of infant care. Together we learned how to take care of the basic needs of my son Matthew. As he grew, my heart expanded as though it would burst with the love I felt for him.

When I became pregnant with my next child during my son's seventh month of life, I panicked. I could not foresee ever having enough love for another child as I had for my son. I suffered from nightmares and panic attacks until my infant daughter lay in my arms. As soon as I held her, I realized something all mothers have come to realize; that the human heart has an infinite capacity for love. We brought her to our trailer home that we shared with our son, and a large German Shepherd dog named Jet. We spent one crowded winter there squeezed together until spring when we rented the farmhouse next door. By then I was already pregnant with my third child. The United States was involved in the Cuban Missile Crisis. We were afraid of a nuclear attack. People around us were building and stocking air raid shelters. The tension was building and I wondered how I could be bringing another life into this chaos.

My life was busy but I lived in fear. We didn't have a working cook stove or a refrigerator in the rambling farmhouse. I learned to cook everything we needed including baking cakes in the electric fry pan. Fortunately, the climate usually supplied refrigeration for most foods but we also kept parishables in the locker cooler. We began construction of our home on a lot behind our butcher shop and freezer-locker business. The years before and those that followed were certainly challenging beyond my comprehension at that time. I cooked noon meals for the hired men during peak business times such as spring and fall in an electric fry pan since we still didn't have a stove. I gave new meaning to the term, "One Dish Meals".

We lived in a rural area where farmers seasonally butchered some of their cattle and hogs to fill their freezers. There was a large deer herd at that time too and the hunting season would find us swamped with work cutting and packaging the venison. Hogs were butchered in the fall before the hunting season began and chickens were slaughtered in the spring. We not only struggled financially but physically as the babies came. The house was constructed to a point where it was barely livable. We built our house without a mortgage because we were both strong and capable but also because of the help of friends and family. We all nailed sub-flooring including our son, who as a three year old became remarkably adept with a hammer. There exist today hundreds of nails in the subflooring of the house that hold nothing but the vigorous energy of a small child with a hammer. He climbed ladders and at least once, fell into the septic tank excavation before it was covered over with dirt. He actually "drove" his Buddy L walk/ride truck down into the septic tank hole. I called and searched for him for a few minutes. I could hear his cries but couldn't tell where he was. There he was scared but unhurt down in the bottom of the hole with his truck.

My mom and dad came as often as they could so dad could help out. I sat on scaffolding hammering nails and painting windows while I was well into my third pregnancy. We didn't have indoor plumbing installed when we moved in, that meant using a chamber pot or trotting down across the yard to our business to use the facilities there. We were searching for a used refrigerator and until we found one, we utilized coolers with ice or the very obliging Vermont out-of-doors. An old wood stove in the basement provided the heat. My husband built hot fires and allowed the heat to come upstairs through the cracks in the sub-flooring. We didn't have the permanent flooring installed so it was like having radiant heat. I can still remember the warmth of those floors that first winter. In fact, in all the houses I have lived in since that time, I have never experienced such comfortable floors as I did in that unfinished structure.

My third child, a girl, was born three and a half weeks early during a cold and raw January. I had slipped and fell hard on the ice twice while feeding the calves, rabbits and pigs. I believe the falls and the incredible fatigue I suffered from were the factors that caused her to come early. She was forced into this dimension by induced labor since my water had broken. In those days the doctors believed the baby had to be born at the time of the water breaking since they didn't approve of dry births. She was born very quickly after the injection of the drugs into my system. Consequently, she was quite blue and had a difficult time breathing immediately after birth. There was also a terrible flu epidemic in our area affecting infants and the elderly. Our little infant daughter was infected as well as our one-year-old daughter. We were able to avoid putting our infant in the hospital but our one-year old child was severely dehydrated and had to be hospitalized. It was an hour drive to the hospital but we wanted to spend as much time with both of our babies as possible. As if the heartache of separation was not enough, I recoil as I remember the shock of seeing my precious toddler restrained with her tiny thighs stuck full of needles as fluid dripped into her system. Each day as I walked onto her floor I could hear her calling out for me. She had been weaned before the hospital stay but one day as I entered her room, she lay on her back, blissfully sucking a bottle balanced on her upraised feet. Somehow we managed to survive this crisis. There would be many more throughout their childhood.

A little over a year and a half later, just before Christmas 1963, I gave birth to my third daughter, my fourth child; a quiet, gentle child who would be pampered by all of us. I spent more time with this child because I didn't have another infant on the way. She was also caught in my postpartum depression that followed her birth and lingered for three years afterward. I was twenty-three years old. I was totally exhausted.

I don't believe I have ever worked as hard physically in my life as I did while caring for my young brood and our business. The fatigue and responsibility took its toll on my emotional well-being and I basically lost all of sense of who I was and why I was here. I began having hallucinations and panic attacks. My ignorance of such matters caused me to hide my symptoms because I feared I would be put away in an institution and lose my children. I could not bear to think of being separated from them. Finally after many months, I dragged myself to my family doctor, told her of my symptoms and confessed my fears. She told me my emotional upheaval was brought on by my high creative nature. Her misdiagnosis would be almost laughable if it wasn't such a serious disorder. Thankfully, she sent me to a mental health clinic where I visited with a social worker twice a week and saw a doctor once a month. Before long, I began to grasp what had happened to me. My discomfort was brought on by fatigue and the hormonal imbalance caused by the births of my four children—Post-Partum Depression. The first words out of the doctor's mouth were, "You are not crazy." Amidst a deluge of tears, the healing process began. Having been cast in the fire of transformation again, I matured from the twenty-three year old child-bride/mother to the strong, capable woman I would become. The workload did not lessen but I approached it from a different perspective. A friend of mine always says there are 360 different ways on the circle of life to view an issue. I have found that if I just step aside and take a look from another angle, my outlook always changes. Nearly every night I was asleep before my head hit the pillow. I slept soundlessly without any obvious dreams unless of course, I had a restless or sick child or two. (Sometimes even three or four at a time) Those were the most difficult to cope with.

By the age of three, it became apparent that my son would need to have his tonsils removed. From the age of one, he was often susceptible to high fevers due to tonsillitis. The fevers resulted in seizures. As an infant he developed a hernia that was surgically repaired. I spent many a restless night checking on his temperature by carefully brushing my lips against his forehead. He was never far from my watchful eyes and senses. My third child also had hernia repair as an infant as well as a tonsillectomy by the age of three. In those days, the doctors believed in removal of the organs instead of treating the whole system of the child. Knowing what I know now, I suspect they both had food allergies. This very same little girl, third child, was born with a congenital femoral rotation inward. By the age of five, her doctor persuaded us to allow him to operate on both long bones of her thighs. They basically severed her legs and put them back on straight. She went to sleep in the hospital free and unrestrained but awakened bound in a full body cast with her legs separated by a broomstick type dowel. She was not prepared for the changes in her body. We weren't either. It was a painful and life-changing experience for her. I was consumed by guilt for consenting to the mutilation and pain that she suffered throughout the surgery and afterwards. We rented a hospital bed, set it up in what was our bedroom. We moved into the den which was nearby. She required round the clock nursing care. The care load was mine to handle. Feeding and entertaining her was the most difficult. She couldn't sit up, so she had to be spoon fed. She balked at every meal and began to lose weight, shrinking in her little cast cage. My other children were very good about playing in the bed with her. Sometimes, though, she would grow impatient and throw everything and everyone out of the bed. A special bond was formed during that time between my children. After three months, she learned to walk all over again on her shaky, thin legs. This was the child who learned to climb upon her rocking horse at seven months and rock it so hard that we weighted it down with heavy catalogs. She walked the first time at eight and a half months. As for me, I was consumed with guilt and loneliness. I was disillusioned with parenthood and life in general. A kind of parent shock descended on my spirit during those years and actually lasted more years than I care to remember. But I managed to stay home with my children until the youngest one went off to school.

After that I found a job in a nearby town as a secretary in a real estate office. That job turned out to be the key to unlocking doors I never dreamed possible for me. I felt alive, vibrant and young once again. I discovered there were many interesting, well-educated people who found me equally interesting and fun to be with. My circle of friends changed and increased in number. I began to socialize with colleagues and clients from the area. There were numerous luncheons and parties to attend. My husband Mac was shy and uncomfortable around my newfound friends. He reluctantly tagged along with me because he knew it was important to me but I know he would have preferred to stay at home. I was moving and growing in experience and worldliness. I hungered for more exposure to this new world I had discovered. I felt that I had finally found my niche. These people didn't think I was odd or different; they seemed to accept me just as I was. I was opening like a beautiful flower to the rest of creation. I was growing up at last. I was twenty-nine years old.

One client loaned me a few classic books, which I devoured as though I were teetering on the brink of starvation. I was back begging for more and that is when I discovered poetry. Every spare moment was spent reading, studying and painting. I dreamed of going to college, of teaching children, of being a famous painter and of traveling all over the world. Many of the people I was surrounded with had traveled extensively and as they shared those experiences with me, I daydreamed. By the third year of my employment and after I had obtained my real estate broker's license, I became increasingly dissatisfied in my marriage and my life in the small farming village. I was earning enough income to support my children and myself when I made the decision to leave my husband and move closer to my new-found friends and my work.

"Change threatens people in many ways,
but those who are growing cannot retreat.
No relationship can stand in the way of growth once it has begun.
The process is inherently bittersweet. The more you grow, the more
people you leave behind." From Invisible Means of Support,
by Dennis Augustine.

SEPTEMBER

Thou abidest within me;
Thou art alive there now;
Thou hast all power;
Thou art now the answer to all I desire;
Thou dost now radiate
Thyself from the center of my being to the circumference,
And out into the visible world as the fullness of my desire.

H.EMILIE CADY, *LESSONS IN TRUTH*

L abor Day finds Duffy and me in Essex, Massachusetts, with my friend, Nicky. Our sister moon appears full and intensely bright. We feel the energy that is being made available to us and we open to it. The light throughout the day seemed different. We are energized and aware of the lightening of our physical bodies as we are raised to another vibratory level of consciousness. We celebrate Labor Day and our combined birthdays by going to the beach, buying bouquets of roses for the house and eating Ben and Jerry's ice cream.

I am overjoyed to be in the presence of my dear friends who generously offered to mentor me through the remaining Polarity classes I need to complete the terminal program of Registered Polarity Practitioner in accordance with the American Polarity Therapy Association standards. Nicky invited me to accompany her to an Applied Kinesiology class for three days on Plum Island. I am very self-conscious in my present state of blindness. Actually, I am quite terrified to meet new people and function in a strange building. I find that when I must totally rely on another person to lead me to my seat, to the bathroom and to lunch, to the car and elsewhere that I feel very fragile and helpless. My sense of self-worth takes a nose dive into a sea of fear and anxiety. I also am tired of explaining my situation each time I meet someone new. It is an odd feeling to be propelled to various places in an automobile and not be able to see the route you came in on. It gives me the sensation that I am flown in and then dropped in a strange place where I must learn to get around, only to be picked up and flown out to be deposited elsewhere. But as she led me in to meet the instructor this morning, I sensed his powerful compassionate presence through his energy field and I felt safe. The group was supportive and I was comforted. The classes are emotionally charged and transforming for many people. For me it is validating to be accepted in a diversified group of my peers in my current state of health.

I have come to realize that a dream I had over and over for many years was actually about me and not my grandmother as I had previously thought. I could see an old woman standing in the darkness way off in the distance, holding a very dim lamp. I felt her loneliness and sadness. A great sense of guilt and sadness would wash over me. Then as I watched her, she slowly moved off waving her lamp and was gone. I always thought the dream was about my grandmother. Now I know that lonely figure in darkness with the lamp at her side was me. I am the old woman in the dream offering the light as a beacon for all those traveling in darkness. I am alone and waiting to guide, to give my wisdom and my love to those who would follow. The sense of hopelessness and sadness that shrouded me was my own inner feelings of abandonment and separation from God.

I have come back to Vermont to stay with my daughter. There are preparations to be made for the wedding of my stepdaughter in Rhode Island towards the end of the month. My family has decided to come together for the sake of their sister but they are uncomfortable at the prospect of being in the same company as my husband and me. There is speculation about his mistress attending. Considering the fact that we are still married, I cannot believe he would bring her to a family affair.

But since he moved in with her back in the spring, he has consistently and prematurely tried to weave her into our family circle. Some of the family members' hackles are high. I am uncomfortable because not only do I have to be in his presence but also his ex-wife and her husband will be there. Once again, there will also be many new people to meet and I will be faced with maneuvering around an old beach hotel. I am going there with closed eyes, which seems very fitting considering the circumstances. I will certainly have selective vision. I pray for guidance and strength to get me through what I see as the final challenge before I head back home to the south.

It is the week before the wedding. I call my husband to make arrangements to go through my books, which are stored nearby. He offers to bring the books to me so I can sort through them. This morning he called to ask if he could bring the first boxes. I am on pins and needles, up early, dressed and waiting. I am alone in the house since my daughter is at work. He pulls up with his truck. I am shaking and crying. I sit down in the living room quietly gathering my sense of self, asking God to stay close by. Joe walks through the door carrying a large box of books that he hastily drops as we both burst into tears. I stand up and he walks into my open arms. We cling together in our shared grief for sometime. He apologizes for his behavior over and over. My mind is whirling. I am confused and so torn. I cannot seem to focus on anything other than this very intense moment. I question him about the woman he is living with and he shrugs it off. I am jolted back into to reality and I begin to think about boundaries and integrity. Then I remember this is the man who walked out on me at the lowest point in my life. Immediately, the energy shifts and I am stronger. After he brings in the remainder of the boxes, he offers to go out for sandwiches. We talk over lunch of family news, a kind of catch-up conversation. He keeps referring to me as "Hon", his old pet name for me. That one word is like a pinch on my arm by my Guidance, reminding me to look beneath the Red Riding Hood mask to the wolf within. He calls later in the afternoon to check on me. The following day, he is back. I decline his offer to drive my daughter and me to Rhode Island to the wedding. Everything is happening too fast. I am in a state of shocked disbelief. I call my attorney who just listens quietly to me and wishes me luck.

My husband asked if I thought we could all be a loving family again at least for the wedding. I will talk with the children and ask them to be open and kind but I cannot speak for their behavior. Reluctantly, I call the children and bring them up to date n the latest news of a possible reconciliation. At the very least, we are once again talking. Each day he calls, offering his assistance and asking to come by. I have finally told him I need time and distance. I tell him this was all too new and was happening too fast for me to deal with. I agree to meet him for a long walk on the beach in Rhode Island.

I am very torn at this point. Parts of me want to just give up, let him take care of me, put it all behind us and go back to the way we were. But the realistic part of me knows there isn't any way back and besides what is back there in the past is not so great anyway. My fears of being disabled, poverty-stricken and alone all came out to do their terrible dance behind my closed eyes. They are very seductive in their attempt to lure me back from God's Light. The weapons I use to defeat those fears are: I feel that my husband will be loyal for a short time and then become angry and resentful once again with my helplessness; I don't feel I can trust him again; And finally, I have come this far with God's help and I am still OK. I realize how much I have grown in the last few months. I can "see" clearly now. I am freer than I had ever been in my life even while being disabled. But even with all the clarity and understanding I am given, I am seriously considering reconciliation. It feels good to have a protective arm around me, the brush of his lips on my cheek, the sense of masculine energy so close. I have been given much to think about in just a few short days.

My daughter and I drive to the wedding arriving a bit later than the others. We share a room overlooking the ocean. Although that may sound *ne plus ultra*, it is situated directly above the band, the very loud 'fifties-type band. As I said, it is an old hotel and lacks sound insulation. Therefore we lay wide-eyed 'til the wee hours virtually rocking and rolling to those fabulous 'fifties tunes. Joe is on hand upon our arrival and has remained the attentive husband throughout my stay. I am pleased to be able to draw on the strength and wisdom of my daughter. She is like an anchor; otherwise, I may be tempted to crawl back in the marriage bed especially after my husband tells me his room is on the other side of the hotel and is quiet.

Early the following day, he knocks on my door and we go off on our beach walk hand in hand. It is very pleasant. I note that for the first time in twenty-six years of being together, we were walking side by side in rhythm with one another. His hand in mine feels very warm and comforting. I fight to keep my mind quiet so I can listen for guidance. I need total awareness. I tell him there is no way I will ever consider reconciliation until he moves into his own place alone. He agrees that he needs to organize his personal life before we can seriously talk about putting our marriage back together. He has set up a meeting with some of our children for tomorrow morning, which seems premature to me.

The wedding ceremony is lovely but I suffer from deep discomfort as my husband grasps my arm and ushers me to a seat next to him. It takes all my inner strength to stay there. Later this evening, I watch as my family once again dances together. It feels so familiar, so comforting to see them all together having fun as they did in the past. I feel like God is showing me what is real and what is illusion but it is up to me to determine which is which.

Monday morning finds me back in my daughter's house in Vermont. Joe has called and asked if he could bring some sandwiches for lunch. We will talk once again. I am excited and anticipate that he will tell me he has moved out of his girlfriend's home as a gesture of his sincere desire to start anew. But when he comes in, he is arrogant and self-serving once more and the first question out of his mouth is, "What percentage of blame do you accept for the failure of this marriage?" I am shocked by his defensive manner. I simply ask, "Where did you sleep last night?" He replies, "You know very well where I slept last night." I ask him to leave and that marks the end of any attempt to reconcile.

I lie down on the sofa and cry tears of humiliation, frustration and pain. I feel battered and bruised by the fall or the way I was pushed off the wild riverboat ride I had been on for a week. An earlier image of Humpty Dumpty falling off the wall comes to mind, as I seem to break into a million fragments. I focus on going home to heal. I call my friend Vera from Raleigh and once again she comes to my rescue. She flies in;

we load the car with dog, cat and stuff and head down the highway the next morning in a cold driving rain.

I repeat the following affirmations several times a day:

1. God is life, love, intelligence, substance, omnipotence, omniscience, and omnipresence.
2. I am a child or manifestation of God, and every moment His life, love, wisdom, power flow into and through me. I am one with God, and am governed by His law.
3. I am Spirit, perfect, whole, and harmonious. Nothing can hurt me or make me sick.
4. God works in me to do His will and He cannot fail.

I have been down in this darkness before and I know the only way out is to lift my eyes upward and seek the Light that is there for me in abundance. In the midst of my process after returning home, I have a powerful dream. I am at a symposium to hear a renowned religious figure speak. He is a great spiritual monk. My husband and my daughters are with me. We find seats towards the back of the auditorium. My husband is sitting behind us. I overhear him telling some people next to him that he and his girlfriend have been trying to buy a house for over a year. I turn to him and tell him how I detest his dishonesty and then I move down in the front. All the seats are taken directly in front, so I sit in the third row center. An announcer came out and tells us that the great one cannot speak today. The young man I am sitting next to turns to me and says, "Come with me, we will go to the great one's home." I am then riding in a white jeep with a group on the way through the desert. It is very beautiful. As we drive, we are given glimpses of the great one driving too. He sees us and we wave to him. He is seated with a white hood over his head. As we round a bend in the road, there bathed in brilliant colors dancing off the rocks and trees, we behold his magnificent home in the caves. I am spellbound.

As I interpret the dream, it is my deepest innermost self that is the great one. That strong male energy is there to lead me through the times when I am unable to receive the direction I wish to hear from outside my self. I will see glimpses of him from time to time if I just keep centering on my heart and my connection to the Earth. I was buoyed by the dream.

As the days go by after my return home, I feel periods of terrible shame—shame for having let myself be tricked into believing that there was hope for a resumption of our relationship. I feel like I have been taken in by a con man. I feel like somehow I should have seen it coming. I have found that having been married as long as I was to one person, that it is very easy to slip back into old behaviors especially when lulled by a sense of comfort and caring. Couples in long-term relationship know exactly what buttons to push and can almost predict the response they will get from their former mate. I talk with some friends about my feelings of shame and guilt. Talking about my feelings really helps. I attend several Emotions Anonymous meetings nearby. The twelve-step group approach has a very positive impact on my emotional adjustment. I soon find that I am not the only person who is powerless over her emotions. I am able to let go of the victim role that I have inadvertently slipped into and begin to pick up the pieces of my life.

Alone outside a church
My heart torn in despair
My future is in question
My dreams all seem to fade
Arms outstretched to heaven
My soul screams out its' pain
I listen as it echoes
And slowly dies away
Simple music fills the air
It lures me to the church
The candles glow so warm
A strange hymn sung so lovely
Slowly I near the choir
Take your place, they tell me
Confused, what part is mine?
A paper handed to me
Inscribed on it "Your Part"
Joy fills me as I read it
It's message all too clear
One word lovingly written
My part, so simple, is FAITH

KATHY JONES, *I HAD A DREAM*

October

O our Father, the Sky, hear us
And make us strong.
O our Mother the Earth, hear us
And give us support.
O Spirit of the East,
Send us your Wisdom.
O Spirit of the South,
May we tread your path of life.
O Spirit of the West,
May we always be ready for the long journey.
O Spirit of the North, purify us
With your cleansing winds.

SIOUX PRAYER

I had signed up a few months before for a Women's Gathering in South Carolina sponsored by a group of native and non-native people called the Bear Tribe. The Bear Tribe was formed early in the 1970's, from a vision beheld by Sun Bear, a sacred medicine man of Chippewa descent who was living near Spokane, Washington. Sun Bear saw a vision of a hilltop bare of trees. A soft gentle breeze was blowing the prairie grass. He beheld a circle of rocks that came out like the spokes of a wheel. Inside this large circle was another circle of rocks, nearer to the center. He knew he was looking at the Sacred Circle, the hoop of his people. Inside the Center Circle was the Buffalo skull, the skull of the Grandmother. As he looked around, he saw coming up through ravines, from the four directions, what at first appeared to be animals. As they came closer, he saw that they were not animals but people wearing headdresses and costumes to honor the animal kingdom. They moved clockwise and made a complete circle before taking their appropriate places on the wheel. He saw in his vision people from all clans, from all the directions of the earth. He also saw that their hearts carried peace. He knew he had to fulfill his vision and hence the Bear Tribe was formed. It grew to be a place where all peoples could come to learn sacred ceremony and how to care for the earth. Although Sun Bear has since gone to spirit, his vision continues through medicine wheel gatherings, pipe carriers' dances, and vision quests taught by others who have been his students. I know of gatherings and teachings being carried on up and down the East Coast. Sun Bear's teachings are also available through his numerous books. (See the suggested reading list in the back of this book)

I become increasingly concerned about traveling anywhere new as my eye condition continues to worsen. The Bear Tribe women who know me encourage me to go along. They assure me there will be plenty of people there to offer a hand. I want to go because I believe it will be a healing experience for me. We will be making drums, singing, dancing and sweating together in the ceremonial sweat lodge. We leave in the predawn hours for the seven-hour trip south to St. Matthews, South Carolina. We are lodged in a beautiful plantation house situated on a slight rise surrounded by tall graceful trees. The house reminds me of the plantation, Tara, in the book, *Gone with the Wind*. I am surrounded by forty like-minded women and I immediately feel welcome and safe. We eat all our meals together in the big dining room seated around a long table. There are always hands ready to help me or to step back as I haltingly shuffle around.

The first evening we spend together in the spacious front room of the old house singing, drumming and telling our stories, grounding the work we will do for the next two days. As I sit at the feet of Wind Daughter, the Medicine Chief, encircled by her beautiful loving energy, warmth spreads through heart. My fears and apprehension are erased and

I am filled with love and peace. The following morning after breakfast, the drum workshop begins. My friend, Nancy volunteers to work with me. We will make my drum first and then hers. The choice of elk hide is random and the one I choose is slightly mottled but disappointingly light in color. Some of the other women choose hides that have definite marks on them that resemble animals or other totems that individualize them and seem to make them special. Pulling the hide across the cedar hoop and lacing it tight is a two-person task. One partner pulls and stretches the hide, holding it tight while the other partner takes up the slack in the rawhide lacing. It can be a delicate process too. If one pulls the lacing too tight, it may break and then have to be spliced back together. As the hide and lacing dry, they tighten around the cedar hoop giving the drum that beautiful resonance of sound. The drums remain silent for one week after they are birthed. I use the term birthed because we sit on the ground facing each other with the drum between our out-stretched legs, gently coaxing the hide tightly over the hoop, in a birthing-like position. A tremendous bond exists after you have pulled a drum with another person. The two drums are also bonded forever. The following morning, I pick up my drum to check on its drying process when I notice on the face of it, the paw marks of the great grizzly bear. A rush of joy sweeps over me as I realize the powerful totem has marked my drum forever.

We have created a harvest altar that consists of autumn vegetables and flowers on the edge of the cornfield. We are each encouraged to carve a jack-o-lantern to add to it for the night's festivities. The carved and lighted pumpkins are then placed in a huge circle around the altar. Several women are gathered on the deck off the kitchen chatting and creating their jack-o-lanterns. I want so much to participate in this creativity but my eyes will not cooperate. For the first time in my life, I feel incapable of creating anything. I can't think of a design and if I could, I can't see to draw on the small vegetable. I make a few holes here and there but I am ashamed to show it to anyone.

We stand in circle, offering our prayers to the six directions; to Creator God, to Earth Mother and then to the four remaining directions of the winds. We pray to the East, to the Spirit Keeper Wabun, to the place of springtime and all that the season promises. Next, we pray to the South, to the Spirit Keeper Shawnodese, place of summer, of bloom, relationship and creativity. This direction is represented by water; the dark, saline feminine aspect of ourselves. The animal associated with the south is the coyote that teaches us to laugh at ourselves and shows us how much we accomplish by chasing our own tail. The third direction is the West, to Spirit Keeper Mudjekeewis who is the Grandfather of all the winds. The West is represented by fire which is transformation and symbolizes the masculine aspect of ourselves. This is the place of autumn and harvest. The grizzly bear symbolizes the West. Finally, we pray to the North and Spirit Keeper Waboose, place of winter and of darkness. The North is where we integrate all that we have learned and accomplished back into the Earth. The White Buffalo Calf symbolizes the North and is honored for bringing the pipe and the sacred tobacco to the Native Americans.

During the sweat lodge this afternoon, I pray for healing for myself. I pray for the Creator's will to be done. I pray for acceptance for whatever is mine to do and experience. I want so much to be a beacon for others who are in similar situations. I pray to be filled with the Christ Consciousness. That is the consciousness of all the teachings of Christ; love, peace, compassion and joy. I weep throughout the powerful cleansing sweat lodge as I feel the spirits of my ancestors gathering around to support my quest.

After our evening meal, we dress in our ceremonial clothing and trek out to the harvest altar where we dance, drum and sing into the night. It seems our circle of women has grown. We are dancing with our grandmothers. Eventually, out of exhaustion, we lie down on our blankets under the stars. I can feel the heat of Earth Mother radiating throughout my body as I stretch out on my thick, woven blanket. The bone-chilling shriek of a screech owl in a tree above my head causes the hair on the back of my neck to rise and sends shivers up my spine. The owl is seen by some Native Americans as a symbol of death and transformation. I believe the owl is here with us to heighten our sensitivity to letting go and beginning again in the death/life cycle. My friend and I, as if on cue, arise and walk slowly through the darkened woods to the house. I dream once again of traveling to the place of the

Great Sage to marvel at the beauty of His home and the excitement of being in His divine presence.

It is dawn; I quietly step out on the porch to meditate in the first rays of the sun. After the last few weeks of emotional devastation, I feel whole, connected and renewed. My life is right on track.

We spend this new morning making drumsticks for our drums. We sit in circle and share our individual experiences of the weekend. I marvel at the love and kindredship that comes with sharing with others in a sacred circle. Many women tearfully open their hearts as they tell their stories. After praying and smoking the sacred pipe, we pack up and head home. We pledge to be in contact with one another throughout the winter and to see each other in the spring at the next Women's Gathering.

Sadly, Halloween comes and goes without celebration. When I lived in the north, we celebrated Halloween with family. My daughter and her family lived in a spacious Victorian house on the main street in our small college town. The first year they lived in the house, she invited us over to share in the trick or treating ritual. So many children came to the door that she ran out of candy and began giving out quarters from rolls they had been saving. The years that followed, the children came in droves. Many dollars were spent on candy and decorations. My other two daughters brought their children to join in the fun. One year, I surprised them by appearing as a giant bear on the porch with my paw out. As I passed into the house with a group of wandering trick or treater's, my son-in-law asked me what I wanted. I did a little dance for him and he offered me the open door but not before one of my daughters looked closely into my bear eyes and announced that those eyes looked so familiar but she couldn't guess who it was. I went out on the porch and sat in their porch swing surrounded by the pumpkins and corn stalks as they all peered out the windows at me. Another group of kids came along and I once again walked into the house with them. I saw the look in my son-in-law's eyes and knew I was pushing my luck. I was about to be booted out on my bear-butt. Suddenly, my small granddaughter looked at me and began to wail in fear. I couldn't bear to see that child cry so I whipped off my headpiece. Each year after that, I appeared as a different large animal but the surprise element of the first time was the height of my masquerading career. When I was a child living in a rural area, we were driven from house to house by our parents. As we became teenagers we were allowed out alone and usually managed to pull a few tricks on some of the residents. My grandmother told us the story of the time the hired man was seated in the outhouse quite comfortably reading the catalog by candlelight when the neighbor boys picked it up and rolled the outhouse down the hill. Luckily no one was injured. When my own children were born my husband and I drove them around from house to house just as my parents did for us. The children would always eat too much candy and, the following week, suffer from stomach distress or colds. My fondness for Halloween at that time of my life was always tempered by the prospect of four children being sick all at once. Rationing of the candy worked to a degree but there was always a certain amount of pilfering that occurred. This year not a single little trickster rings my bell and I say another goodbye to the past.

Since I now have a tentative diagnosis, I have begun to explore it on the Internet. I have discovered so much about this disease I am experiencing. The generic name for this type of disease is dystonia. There are many different types of dystonia. The word dystonia describes abnormal involuntary sustained muscle contractions and spasms. One of them is Focal Blepharospasm that pertains to the eyes. Dystonia is a neurological movement disorder. It is frequently misunderstood by the public and often misdiagnosed by the medical profession because of its complexity. Dystonia results in sustained muscle contractions frequently causing twisting and repetitive movements or abnormal postures. It may affect one or several parts of the body and it is frequently painful. Blepharospasm is a condition where there is sustained, forced, involuntary closing of the eyelids. It is both a cranial and a focal dystonia. Blepharos comes from the Greek word for eyelids. Cranial refers to the head and focal indicates confinement to one part. Patients with blepharospasm have normal eyes and, as in my case, often have excellent acuity. The visual disturbance is due solely to the forced closure of the eyelids. Blepharospasm usually begins gradually with excessive blinking and/ or eye irritation. In the early stages it may only occur with specific precipitating stressors, such as bright lights, fatigue, driving, watching

TV, and emotional tension. As the disease progresses, it occurs more frequently during the day. The spasms relax during sleep and often after sleep don't reappear for several hours after waking. Concentrating on a specific task often temporarily reduces or relieves the spasms. As in my case, singing, yawning or speaking to someone about a subject that I am particularly passionate about would miraculously eliminate the spasms. I think some people believe I am faking because one minute my eyes are shut tight as I listen to them. When it is my turn to respond, my eyes snap open wide and bright. One man I contacted who suffers from blepharospasm said he found it interesting to sit in meetings while his eyes were involuntarily shut tightly. The others thought he was asleep and he overheard some interesting comments. As for me and many others with blepharospasm, the spasms may intensify so that the eyelids may remain frequently closed for several hours at a time.

Blepharospasm is thought to be due to abnormal functioning of the basal ganglia, which are situated at the base of the brain. The basal ganglia play a role in all coordinated movements. No one seems to know what goes wrong in them. It is thought that there is a disturbance in the various "messenger" chemicals involved in transmitting information from one nerve cell to another. Occasionally, a history of eye trauma may exist but usually it develops quite spontaneously with no known precipitating factor. In my case, I have experienced several head and neck injuries during my years as an equestrian. The first occurred with I was 9 years old. As I galloped down a rocky slope bareback on Duke, he stumbled and fell down. I was thrown under him and knocked out. When I roused, he was standing over me sniffing my face. My blue jeans were torn from the ankle to the crotch on the leg he had stepped on. I had "borrowed" my older sister's new white fur lined boots without her permission. My injuries were nothing compared to facing her wrath. My arm had a large abrasion on it and would become infected. I had a partial hoof print on my ribs too. I gathered myself and the horse to hobble to Grandma's house. She took one look and ordered me to bed. Then she called my mother and father. I remember the anxiety of waiting for them to come. My father threatened to kill the horse and forbade me to ride again. Long story short, that threat was never carried out and I was back riding in a few days.

Infrequently, it is a familial disease with more than one family members affected. Blepharospasm can occur along with dystonia involving other parts of the body, such as, oromandibular dystonia or Meige syndrome which affects the muscles of the mouth and/or jaw. This consists of clenching of the jaw, opening the mouth and/or involuntary protrusion of the tongue. Blepharospasm can be induced by certain medications such as those used in Parkinson's disease. Usually, the symptoms disappear with a reduction or adjustment in the medication. Much of the information I have written here was gleaned from the Dystonia Medical Research Foundation in Chicago, Illinois. Their website is www.dystonia-foundation.org.

Many times patients with blepharospasm become socially isolated because they fear the social scrutiny as well as the clumsiness and inability to move without assistance during times of spasm. I have found that to be very true in my case. I cannot walk alone especially in strange areas. A great deal of pressure is on me when I go grocery shopping. I either hang onto someone else or onto a cart allowing myself to be guided around. If I attempt to go it alone, I go very slowly because there is a good chance I will hit someone else. I have had some close calls. Most people joke about it good-naturedly because they don't realize that I had just blinked and my eyes didn't reopen for a length of time. I often run into displays or knock items from shelves. I am a virtual bull in the china shop. There is also the feeling that I need to explain to people why I have my eyes closed or am pouring eye drops into my eyes at regular intervals—drops that often flow down my cheeks and nose so I am mopping myself up with a tissue. Most of the time, I have a pocket full of eye drop empties on the left side and a pocket full of usable ones on the right side. I am totally dependent on the artificial tears. I have found that wearing my colored glasses helps to mask my eyes from the public and also cuts down on the glare from the overhead fluorescent lights that seem to burn through one's brain. One of my most stressful times during shopping is paying the bill and writing the check. I become so tense that my eyes refuse to open. I push them open only to have them resist even harder. I am offered a check card or debit card at my local bank and that saves me much aggravation at the check-out counter.

Occasionally, I go out with people I don't know too well. As we walk side by side from their cars to where we are going, suddenly my eyes go into spasm and I stop short. I have learned the hard way to stop and not try to move forward because there is a chance I will bump into something or fall flat on my face. I hesitate and wait, not so patiently, until my eyes decide to give me their benefit. In the meantime, the party or parties with me have moved well out of the way when they realize that I am left behind. Most of the time, it makes a good laugh, rarely is it an awkward situation. The alternative to going out, that is staying home alone, is unappealing to me.

Consequently, I find that I force myself to go out and be amongst people even though I know that I will face situations that may be embarrassing and stressful. Some people are not comfortable talking to me face to face when my eyes are closed or in spasm. Our disease creates dis-ease in others. It actually means a great deal to us to be treated as we were before we developed this disease. And, yes, we do appreciate the offer of a hand as we struggle along.

> *At night make me one with the darkness.*
> *In the morning make me one with the Light.*
> WENDELL BERRY

NOVEMBER

Thirteen months later

S acred stones like cairns along the road litter my pathway. I see each one and remember, yes, I lived there. They are like familiar old friends roadside shrines that bring me comfort as I pass by them.

This book is intended as a yearlong diary of transformation, this chapter treats of a thirteenth month, a baker's dozen. It is also about the circle of life, of death, dying and rebirth. In numerology and in reading the tarot cards, I have been told I carry the number 13. Thirteen is about transformation; death and rebirth. Like the setting of the sun, death of the old patterns must come to allow for the promise of renewal and rebirth upon the wings of the Glory Glow sunrise. The native people believe in the influence of the Thirteenth Moon. The Thirteenth Moon is a time of great flux, of transition and new opportunity. It is a time of questioning everything you might have previously believed, a time of deep and lasting change on some or all levels of your being.

In the circle of life, it is the winter or the North, the place of the Spirit Keeper, Waboose, of the White Buffalo Woman. Many people ask who is White Buffalo Woman. One version of the native legend that was told to me is that she is a spirit woman who goes by many names in many tribes. She is part of the sacred feminine principle of the Creator. White Buffalo Woman brings the knowledge of life, birth, and death; the practice of healing; understanding the feminine cycles; the first medicine; the sacred pipe; the sweat lodge; and many of the most sacred of ceremonies. The legend goes that the tribes were camped, there wasn't any game and they were starving. Two young scouts were sent out to look for buffalo. As they scanned a hill in the distance, they saw something coming toward them. The figure appeared to be floating not walking. They knew whatever this was, it was Holy. The figure came close and the young men realized it was a beautiful woman. The most beautiful woman they had ever seen. She carried a bundle with her and a fan of sage leaves. She shone with light and power. One young man was in awe of her and stood back. The other lusted after her body and reached out to touch her. Because she was Holy, touching was not allowed and the scout was immediately struck by lightning. There was nothing but a pile of burned bones on the ground. White Buffalo Woman told the remaining awestruck young man to go forth, tell his chief to prepare a ceremonial place for her coming. The young scout ran back to the chief and advised him of what he had witnessed. The people built a sacred teepee for their visitor. She carried with her the sacred pipe and instructed the people in the sacred pipe ceremony as well as other ceremonies. She taught the women and the children how to live and pray. She gave them all hope and prophesy.

As she left from the direction she had come, she stopped and rolled over three times. The first time, she turned into a black buffalo; the second time into a brown one; the third time into a white female buffalo calf. A white buffalo is the most sacred living thing on earth. As soon as she had disappeared over the hill, the buffalo came in droves sacrificing themselves to the people for their survival. The buffalo gave the people everything they needed and are therefore considered sacred. The North is also the place of the cold winds and a time to go deep into dormancy or quiet to enable us to integrate all that we have learned thus far along the circle of life back into Earth Mother. This is where we prepare to emerge on the other side; reborn, refreshed and ready to begin again in the spring or energy of Wabun, Spirit Keeper of the East.

Old cells constantly die within our bodies to make room for the new. Scientists tell us that every seven years, our bodies are totally recreated allowing us the opportunity to grow and change. We also create who we are and who others are by our thoughts and beliefs. By changing our minds and our thought forms, we can actually change our structure and image, as well as others. We can change the consciousness and raise the vibration of others by how we view them, by our thoughts of them. Each thought is a prayer. We must take responsibility for them. Thoughts go out into the Universal Consciousness or energy field as a vibration which will affect the vibration of the whole. Much like a pebble dropped in a quiet pond will eventually affect all life in the pond and then become part of the pond so do our thoughts. Therefore, when we think judgmental thoughts of others, we are lowering the vibration of the whole. For instance, you see a bag person or a beggar on the street corner. You focus your thoughts on how awful, how disgusting, how shameful that person is. You will see their shoulders slump a little deeper as the energy created by your negative vibrational thoughts affect the energy field around them. If you can surround them with Light and realize that they are created as you are but are at a different place in their journey, you will raise not only the individual's vibration, but also the vibration of all who are at that same place.

We are all in a state of transition. We are like actors in a grand production. As we near the final act, the spectacular, most important part of this great creation, I urge everyone to let go of fear. There are those who are selling fear to the public through films and books. The coming Ascension is not the end of the world but the beginning. Instead of buying into the fear, look deeply into your heart and allow that expansion. Right now as we approach the end of the Mayan Calendar, everyone feels the need to be in the correct place next to the appropriate person on this grand stage we call life. Perhaps, we wish to stand alone during the time of transition. There is no right or wrong. All that is required is an open heart. We are seeing many changes in our lives and those around us as people adjust to their proper places. This final act will be the mass ascension of the entire population to another higher dimension. The ascension process is referred to by many Christians as the Second Coming of Christ. There are those who believe that Christ will appear from the heavens and take various selected people with Him to some glorious place. What about all the other devout believers? To me, the coming of Christ occurs when each individual raises their awareness (vibration) of the Christ Consciousness (the teachings of

Jesus, realizing that His most important teaching was our connectedness with all God has created). To ascend, we must accept our own Divinity. The illusion of separation, judgment, and superiority must disappear as well as our fear of death. We will see all of creation as part of ourselves and we will once again walk gently and respectfully on this Earth. I believe the acceptance of the Christ within each of us will occur at a rapidly increasing pace. Many of us have already ascended to a higher vibrational plain and are teaching others to follow. We are holding the Light for those that come after us. It becomes easier for those who follow in the steps already carved in the path by those who have gone before. As we reach critical mass in our Ascension process, the pace will quicken again. In the meantime, it may seem as though the world is "going to hell in a hand basket" as the dark side, the negative thoughts fight back harder than ever in the face of the increased Light. We are all experiencing the quickening now. Very soon, most of us will ascend to another higher dimension; a dimension of lightness, beauty, peace and love. We will be capable of restoring our beautiful planet to health and wholeness. The Earth will be a planet of Light and Love as it was intended by the Creator. The use of new forms of earth friendly energy will become known to us. That is already happening on a daily basis. Our food sources will be pure and nutritious once again. We will not have to take the life of another for any reason. I have been witnessing the changes in the newborn infants for sometime. They are being born with heightened awareness and carry intense Light within their cells. They are being born prepared for the ascension process. They will lead us in learning to Love one another.

Surely, the Goddess lives again through our Inner Light. Every change brings about opportunity for rebirth. This is God's perfect plan for us. Filling our minds with love-thoughts, I don't mean the Hallmark variety; I mean positive heart-felt energy of the non-judgmental kind. Seeing each change as an opportunity for positive growth can fill us with love-thoughts, which will cast out all fear of death. Through this wisdom we can overcome death. Death is the ultimate birth.

Sometimes we need to be motivated through sickness or pain to allow the transformation of our minds to take place. We become so distracted by the illusions of worldliness in which we surround ourselves that we don't listen to that still small voice within. If we can open ourselves each day, to the everyday opportunities for growth that we are given, then perhaps we can avoid the devastating lessons that we receive as a result of not accepting or listening to the whispers of that small voice within. That is when we are pushed by the more difficult lessons, what I identify as "the two-by-four wake-up call", the not so gentle voice that stops us short and forces us to either change and grow or continue on in our ego-centered state gradually going deeper and deeper into darkness. The loud wake-up call lessons offer us immensely powerful opportunities for growth. We will always experience despair and pain as we journey through these growth surges and perhaps we will not physically survive the ordeal but we can still chose to be healed spiritually even though we may shed our physical form. We have the free will to choose a light-filled spirit that will provide us with peace and a sense of our purpose here in this life or we can chose to allow darkness to condemn our spirit to unprecedented pain, suffering and lack of peace forevermore. We can choose to be elevated by a tragic event in our lives or we can choose to be crushed by it. We can also move through our lessons with more love thoughts and more creativity instead of sitting back waiting for the lessons that utilize struggle. We can ask for gentle lessons as we open to Spirit's voice. We need not carry our lessons with us as we climb the ladder to greater consciousness. In fact, we must drop them as we complete each one, otherwise our load would be so heavy, and we would not be in a position to climb any further. We need not take the steps we have trod with us either as they should remain behind for others to follow. We have carved out the path and marked it for others who will come behind us. That too is part of our service.

As we age, we feel the necessity to shed the material goods we have accumulated along our journey. I suggest we not only shed the material items but also the lessons we have been clutching to our hearts with such fear. We fear we will forget our lessons especially the "hard ones". The fact is, we will not forget what is important and we will not repeat them. We must keep our burdens light as we open wider towards the acceptance of the All One—the Great I Am.

This transformation has taught me to connect to my inner-self, to see within by removing the outer stimulus. I am born of fire. My spirit has been tempered by the fire of transformation many times during my life. I have felt the presence of Mudjekeewis, Spirit Keeper of the West, in the form of the great grizzly bear, teaching me how to sift through the accumulated baggage to reveal all that is necessary for my spirit to shine. I have learned to go deep within myself all the while reexamining and redefining who I am; why am I here and what do I need in this life? Learning to breathe deeply while allowing the breath of life to open and cleanse my system. I realized recently that I have never claimed my-self. I have always been someone's daughter, mother, wife, lover, teacher, employee, grandmother but never just me. I tried to write about who I am and I find I cannot do so without using others to define who I am. Although the support of others is necessary when one embarks on a journey of spiritual healing.

I am grateful to the many women who have come to my side throughout my life. Attending the spring Women's Gathering for the second time, was equally as powerful for me as it was when I was blind. I attended with improved sight due to the botox injections I had again received in March. Meeting all my sisters whose voices I remembered but whose faces I hadn't clearly seen was very moving for me. I soared through the weekend with little wings of joy on my heels

Early in this journey I was given the "D" words; discipline, discovery, discernment and detachment, in that order as a matter of fact. The lessons continue over and over in each one of these "D" word courses along the way. I must repeat the "discovery" lesson again by redefining who I really am. I am a work in progress.

Discipline applies to conditioning the mind to right thinking by the use of positive, constructive and divine thoughts, words and feelings. We must learn to take responsibility for our thoughts, feelings and words. Where our thoughts are is where we are. We are responsible for the feeling behind our chosen words and thoughts because the power of love gives them life, a higher vibratory frequency. Conversely, words and thoughts that are negative and dark given with great conviction will lower the vibration of the whole consciousness, bringing violence, war, disease and destruction. Negative words, feelings, thoughts and conditions carry only the power that we the individual give to them. If we eliminate the negative from our vocabulary, change our thought processes to thoughts of love, we will change the planet. There will be no violence against anyone or anything. World hunger will disappear along with war and disease. Sounds simplistic? Yes, it actually is! If everyone on the planet would ask themselves one question throughout the day, "What would an emissary of love do now?"

It begins with our leaders, our teachers and our clergy, and then it filters down. The example I used earlier in the book of the ripples in the pond effect is helpful in understanding this concept. As thoughts, words and actions of love, of a Divine nature are given out or dropped in the still pond of human consciousness, the ripples flow outward in concentric circles affecting the entire body of beings. Imagine a newscast without violence. Check out most of the TV shows the newscasts or movies available today for children and adults. Much of the violence we watch is perpetrated against women and children. We have our free will to turn our backs and walk away, turn off the set, refuse to see the movies, in other words, give no power to the negative vibrations, they will completely disappear to be replaced with love, grace, peace and joy—replaced by our Divinity. We have the power and the ability to create what we want through discipline of our words and thoughts.

As St. Paul once said, "Pray incessantly." Make each thought an appropriate prayer by training the mind to focus on God—on righteousness, "right-use-ness." There is no higher vibratory word than the word, "God". Repeating the word, God as many times a day as possible will bring in thoughts of a higher frequency. Look for the face of the Christ in every person you meet, surround them in Light. Allow time each day to communicate with God through prayer and meditation. Sit in the energy of your Highest Self, your Highest Inner Knowing, and listen. God's voice can only be heard in silence.

Discovery applies to the realization that we are Divine. The acceptance of our own Divinity and therefore, our perfection will allow us to manifest anything at any time. Discovering the teachings that have been written by those who have gone before will show us the Truth. Whether the teaching is Hindu, Judaism, Christian or metaphysics, the true message is found in the human heart. Wherever we are at the moment is the correct place for us to find the truth when we listen to our heart. We must look for the Truth at the Source and the Source will be found within our hearts.

The lesson in Discernment is an ongoing lesson. It is a lesson of boundaries. My teacher, Kiyo Sasaki Monro, in her book, *Love and Hope,* describes the process of discernment as follows: First, take a deep breath, pushing out all preconceived ideas to allow the appropriate information to flow in. Affirm your intention to avoid being influenced by the source of the information you are receiving. Secondly, check the information for any ego or self-serving motivation on the part of the source. Third, accept only that which is given with a positive, loving attitude, and which gives you courage and power to live your life even in the face of difficulties. Eliminate all judgment, blame or criticism. Do not allow fear or intimidation to enter into your discernment process. Fourth and most importantly, take the information into your heart and determine whether it resonates there and whether it brings you joy. Avoid allowing the mind to evaluate the information. Listen carefully to your Superconscious Self whispering guidance through your open heart. Once you have discerned your truth, especially if the information goes against the accepted ideas of others in the world, living your truth takes genuine courage.

Detachment lessons have been hard earned for me. There have been many changes in my family during the last ten years. We have survived and reunited but we are different from before. We are stronger individuals. We stand in our own power but we are united by our love and respect for one another. There is no one in our family group that has not been touched by the changes not even the newborn and the soon—to-be-born. We continue to grow towards the Light.

The other word I have recently received, and have not included in the above list is "disability". It is a word that I do not accept. I do not want to categorize myself as dis-abled, thereby owning it. I don't feel that I am in denial (coincidentally another "D" word) but to name my physical challenge as a disabling dis-ease is to claim it as my own. I do claim my Perfection, my Divinity and my service. I have prayed for many years to be of service to my fellow brothers and sisters. Now I finally realize that I am serving the will of God by accepting who

I am right now with grace and joy. I pray daily for those who are spiritually, emotionally and physically blinded. Through the expansion of my prayers, many will feel the increased Light and love of my Christ Consciousness. The ripples flow outward from me and back again expanding in ever-widening circles, touching and thereby raising the vibration of Light for all. I am willing to adjust my life to allow for whatever limitations are given me but I am not dis-abled according to God's Law of unending service.

> *That which God said to the rose,*
> *And caused it to laugh in full-blown beauty,*
> *He said to my heart,*
> *And made it a hundred times more beautiful.*
> MATHNAWI III, 4129

Afterward

In looking backwards as I am wont to do before proceeding onward, I look behind to see the ghosts of those who have walked with me for awhile. They have been my teachers, advisors, friends and fellow story tellers. I have left them behind or they have disappeared from my life. They are my tribe which I have created along this journey. They appear like those monuments along our roadways where people have died in accidents. How do I reconcile those losses that have so deeply affected my heart song? Tears sting my face but I revel in being able to move forward. I am eager to build my tribe again from those I will meet on this new path. A strong voice reverberates within my soul, "Live in the layers, not in the litter". I am not finished with my transformation.

I cannot adequately explain the discomfort and difficulty surrounding the year before I finally found an answer regarding my near blindness. I sat in front of many doctors explaining my symptoms while they looked directly into my wide-open eyes with disbelief and doubt. As soon as I would finish speaking, my eyes would snap shut and have to be pried open with my fingertips. I told them how my eyes would open freely and stay open when I sang at the top of my lungs. I used this technique when I was driving or kayaking. I became known around here as the singing kayaker as I paddled around the river in the early morning hours. When I couldn't think of a song, I made one up. I actually sang my story to the river many times. Those early doctors didn't have a clue and were as much in the dark as I. Whenever I became passionate about anything during a conversation, my eyes were wide open. I found that hugs from friends and loved ones alleviated my spasms for the duration of the hug and sometimes afterward for awhile. I think many people thought I was faking it or had an emotional illness. There were times when I might have agreed with them as I could find no explanation for my bizarre behavior. I have been fortunate to have been surrounded by many loving friends. I have been the recipient of much compassion and love. For many others, this disease causes isolation from the outside world. It is uncomfortable having to explain to others why I am sometimes blind and at other times, not so blind. Often blinking, shaking my head and always pouring artificial tears into my eyes. Much of the artificial tears flow back out and down my cheeks. It becomes a blinking, scowling, pouring, mopping ritual repeated over and over almost continuously. The tears I use come in individual prepackaged vials that require one to twist off the tiny top. My mother once remarked that she would always be able to find me from my trail of little plastic tear tops.

I approach my appointment at the University of North Carolina at Chapel Hill with a sense of eager anticipation. I am determined that no fear of any kind will creep into my mind to dampen my enthusiasm for treatment. Now that I finally have a diagnosis, surely the Botoxin injections that will weaken the muscle contractions in my lids will alleviate the symptoms. I am ready to be reborn with new sight. My appointment is scheduled for December 1. I would receive multiple Botoxin injections around the bony orb of each eye, which is the location of the muscles responsible for blinking. Coincidentally, I have decided to give a "Thanks for Giving" party on December 7 for eighteen people who have helped me throughout the last nine months. I am very excited about doing something special for these people who have given me so much support and love. I hire a caterer and we plan the menu along with some special autumn touches.

I found out the Botoxin will not take effect for approximately seven to ten days after injection, I wonder if the party will be an "eye opener". Perhaps we will truly have much to celebrate. The Creator has a wonderful sense of humor and appreciates a celebration so on the seventh day not only was there rest from the labors of creation as portrayed in the Bible but there is a party at my house.

Early this morning I noticed a difference in the amount of time my eyes stay open and I am not blinking constantly in spasm. By the time the guests arrive, we truly have reason to celebrate. It is a Thanks For Giving party for those that stood by me and allowed me to remain in my home during my personal rebirthing process but it is also a Thanks to God party for giving me back the use of my eyes.

As the days pass, it becomes even more miraculous to me. I am as a child not knowing what I want to do first. I want to see and feel everything anew. Each day is a celebration of life and love, of renewal and rebirth, of resurrection. I believe the true meaning of the resurrection of Christ, is the ultimate victory over death of self, self-bondage and the conception of separation from God.

When I first became aware of my spiritual journey of awakening, I prayed to let go of self and give my life over entirely to God's plan for me. I eventually felt I had accomplished that cleansing process and was truly guided by my Creator. But actually it was my strong, clever and resistant ego that created that illusion so thoroughly and believably. Some aspects of my being had been turned over to God's guidance and control but my relationship with my husband and myself was totally in the grip of my tenacious ego. There was an absence of balance in my life. There was dishonesty and deceit stemming from fear, which is the absence of love. I could not hear the voice of God over the sound of fear. Had I not been so blind, even before I was actually blind, I would have seen that I was opening myself up for the major "two-by-four" lessons of discernment and detachment.

O Lord, I have long been engrossed in material things.
Enthralled by their outward forms,
I failed to perceive within them Thy creative Spirit.
The starry single eye of my soul insight.
PARAMAHANSA YOGANANDA, *WHISPERS OF ETERNITY*

During these last few years, I have worked through major lessons, not alone but with the help of the Divine Spirit. There have been many teachers, some have become friends. There have been those who taught me the most difficult lessons too. I am grateful for them but also equally as grateful that they are gone. One day after these chapters were written, I sat around a table with a group of friends. We were discussing last year, 1998. There were so many stories of personal tragedy, sickness, financial failure and painful lessons. I opened my mouth to comment and was as surprised as my friends were by what I uttered. I said, "This has been such a great year for me." I realized then how blessed I am for having come this way. I also realized the strength and sunny beauty of my spirit. Every cell of my body felt as though it was filled with light. I felt embodied by the Christ Light. I am truly standing in the stream of this life prepared to accept whatever role God offers me.

"God in me is infinite wisdom; I know just what to do."
H. EMILIE CADY, *LESSONS IN TRUTH*

A year and a half after the decision was made to drop out of the Polarity Realization Institute, I was able to complete my studies and become a Registered Polarity Practitioner. The only way I could have completed the program was with the help of two very special friends, Nicky and Elaine. They had faith in my ability to learn the work, sense the energy and utilize my healing touch with clients despite the blindness that had overtaken me by this time.

When we receive these major life lessons that bring about great transitions in our lives, we must remember that God will lead us higher than we ever dreamed we could go if we just let go of our fears and our discouragement. If we become too fearful and hang on to our old ways or our lessons, not allowing ourselves to die and go into the ground, nothing grander can come from our suffering. We may miss the lesson entirely and remain in a state of dis-ease for the remainder of our life here on earth. If we let go, we will receive God's greatest gift to us, the gift of resurrection, of newness of life and of springtime. If we turn to embodying the Christ-consciousness within ourselves rather than continuously focusing on the results then the healing rebirth will occur as if by magic. As Jesus dictated in The Course In Miracles, "When you perform a miracle, I will arrange both time and space to adjust to it." Jesus also offered the following parable in one of his sermons. I am not quoting it exactly. When a farmer plants a field of wheat, the weeds grow along with the wheat seeds. They are both seeds and one can see them as life experiences, good and evil, light and darkness. If we try to pull up the weed seedlings, we will no doubt pull up the wheat plants as well. Better to let them grow up together until harvest. After harvest, we can sort through the accumulation and pull out the unwanted, undesirable weeds, tossing them into the fire of transformation. We are left with the beautiful heart of the life-giving wheat, the fine shining gold. We have come full circle once again and are born of the fire.

Allowing ourselves to "die to self" means letting go of our past entirely. Just erasing it and beginning anew. A Course in Miracles teaches us that in being born again, in letting go of the past, we can look without condemnation on the present. We are asked to let go of the future by placing it in God's hands. We will then see by our experiences that we have lain the past and present in His hands as well, because the past will punish us no more and all-future dread will be meaningless. That is in my opinion, the true meaning of relief from the bondage of self.

In my healing practice, I often see bands surrounding a client's energy field. These individuals are bound so tightly; they feel great pain everywhere especially in their connective tissue. Their breathing is shallow and labored. The Life Force cannot possibly flow through their energy field to nurture their biology. These are the bands of fear from past experiences, past trauma, and old thought forms. When these bands are released in whatever way is appropriate, miracles happen. People get well, they become reborn. Carlos Castaneda writes in his book, *Tales of Power* about his teacher, Don Juan, who at one point says to his student, "One day, I discovered I didn't need personal history, so like drinking, I just dropped it." Easier said than done, in that people who know us and know our personal history have developed expectations of us. Expectations can become resentments very quickly. The answer is realizing the truth, that no one has power over us unless we allow it.

In the Gnostic Gospel of St. Thomas, Jesus says, "There is within you that which will redeem you if you bring it forth, or destroy you if you do not bring it forth. If you run from anguish, you will live a life of anguish; but if you are willing to dive into it and bring it forth, you will be liberated in truth." And Jesus goes on to say, "If you know how to suffer, you do not suffer; if you know how to die, you do not die." That is what I mean when I say, meet your greatest fear. Meet your emotions and your anguish. In short, meet your Karma. Don't do battle with your emotions or your past, just meet it and let it go. Karma, I believe, means opportunity and challenge.

As I write this afterward, several years have passed since I received that first set of Botoxin injections. I have had many more sets given at three month intervals. The results are always uncertain but I continue to seek relief and pray for a cure. I have had to deal once again with disappointment but throughout I have continued to grow in spirit. Five years after this year long diary, I did finally drive again and yes, rode my bike too. After enduring three hurricanes alone, I sold my beautiful NC home and moved to Virginia to be closer to family. Mr. Duffy passed away at age sixteen and Perceval five months later of cancer. As my vision improved and my sense of freedom was reborn, I sold that house and moved into a motor home. My present dog, a rescue pup named Sebastian and I took to the gypsy life quite well for four more years. Then I felt the need to settle once again. I bought a cottage in the Adirondack foothills where we now live and work. On May 6, 2010, tragedy struck when my beloved son Matthew was killed by a falling tree and I am now faced with another thrust into the fire of transformation.

Let me always be guided,
Guarded, and directed.
Let my meditations be consistent with
What God would have me be,
That I may illustrate in my relationships
With others, the fact that
The Christ walks and talks with me.

DEANNA COTTRELL, *MY PRAYER*

Born Of Fire
Suggested Reading List

Dancing With The Wheel by Sun Bear, Wabun Wind and Crysalis Mulligan; Fireside Books, Simon and Schuster, Rockefeller Center, 1230 Avenue of the Americas, NY, NY 10020; copyright 1991

Black Dawn, Bright Day by Sun Bear with Wabun Wind; Fireside Books, Simon and Schuster, Rockefeller Center, 1230 Avenue of the Americas, NY, NY10020; copyright 1992

God Calling edited by A.J.Russell, Jove Books, Dodd, Mead & Company, The Berkley Publishing Group, 200 Madison Ave., NY, NY 10016; 1978

Lessons in Truth by Emilie Cady—Unity Books, Unity Village, Missouri; No date information

Love & Hope by Kiyo Sasaki Monro; Oughten House Publications, POBox 2008, Livermore, CA 94551; 1997

American Indian, Myths and Legends by Richard Erdoes and Alfonso Ortez; Pantheon Books, Div. of Random House, Inc., NY, NY ; 1984

Your Sacred Self by Dr. Wayne W. Dyer; Harper Collins Publishers, Inc., 10 East 53rd St., NY, NY 10022; 1995

Deep Water Passage by Ann Linnea; Pocket Books, Div. of Simon & Schuster, Inc., 1230 Ave. of the Americas, NY, NY 10020; 1993

Whispers From Eternity by Paramahansa Yogananda; Self-Realization Fellowship, 3880 San Rafael Ave., Los Angeles, CA 90065; 1993

Autobiography Of A Yogi by Paramahansa Yogananda; Self-Realization Fellowship, 3880 San Rafael Ave., Los Angeles, CA 90065; 1993

Earth Prayers From Around The World, edited by Elizabeth Roberts and Elias Amidon; Harper Collins Publishsers, 10 East 53rd Street, NY, NY 10022

Black Elk Speaks as told through John G. Neihardt; University of Nebraska Press, Lincoln, Nebraska; 1998

A Course In Miracles from the Foundation For Inner Peace, published by the Foundation For Inner Peace, PO Box 598, Mill Valley, CA 94942; 1992

Life and Teachings of the Masters of the Far East by Dr. Baird T. Spalding; Published by DeVorss & Company, PO Box 550, Marina delRey, CA 90294; 1964

The Polarity Process by Franklyn Sills; Element Books, Inc., PO Box 830, Rockport, MA 01966

The Books by Alice A. Bailey, a complete list available through Lucas Publishing Company, 113 University Place, Cooper Station, NY, NY 10276; 1997

Rolling Thunder by Doug Boyd; Dell Pub. Co., ISBN: 038528859X; reissue edition

Rolling Thunder Speaks by Rolling Thunder; Edited by Carmen Sun Rising Pope; ClearLight Publishers, 823 Don Diego, Santa Fe, NM 87501; 1999

Mystics, Magicians And Medicine People by Doug Boyd; Marlowe and Company, 632 Broadway, Seventh Fl, NY, NY 10012; 1989

Mad Bear by Doug Boyd; Touchstone, Simon & Schuster Building, Rockefeller Center, 1230 Avenue of the Americas, NY, NY 10020; 1994

The Initiation by Dr. Donald Schnell; Element Books, Inc., 160 North Washington St., 4th Floor, Boston, MA 02114; 2000

In The Spirit Of Business by Robert Roskind; Celestial Arts Publishing, P O Box 7123, Berkeley, CA 94707; 1992

Invisible Means Of Support by Dr. Dennis F. Augustine; Golden Gate Publishing,; ISBN: 0963673602; 1994

Gifts Of Spirit by Dr. Dennis F. Augustine, Heartsfire Books, 500 N. Guadalupe St., Suite G-465, Santa Fe, NM 87501;1997

The Nag Hammadi Library, James M. Robinson, General Editor; HarperCollins Publishing, 10 East 53rd St., NY, NY 10022; 1990

Why Me, Why This, Why Now by Robin Norwood; Carol Southern Books, 201 East 50th St., NY, NY 10022; 1994

Animal Speak by Ted Andrews; Llewellyn's New Worlds of Mind and Spirit, PO Box 64383-028., St. Paul, MN 55164; 1996